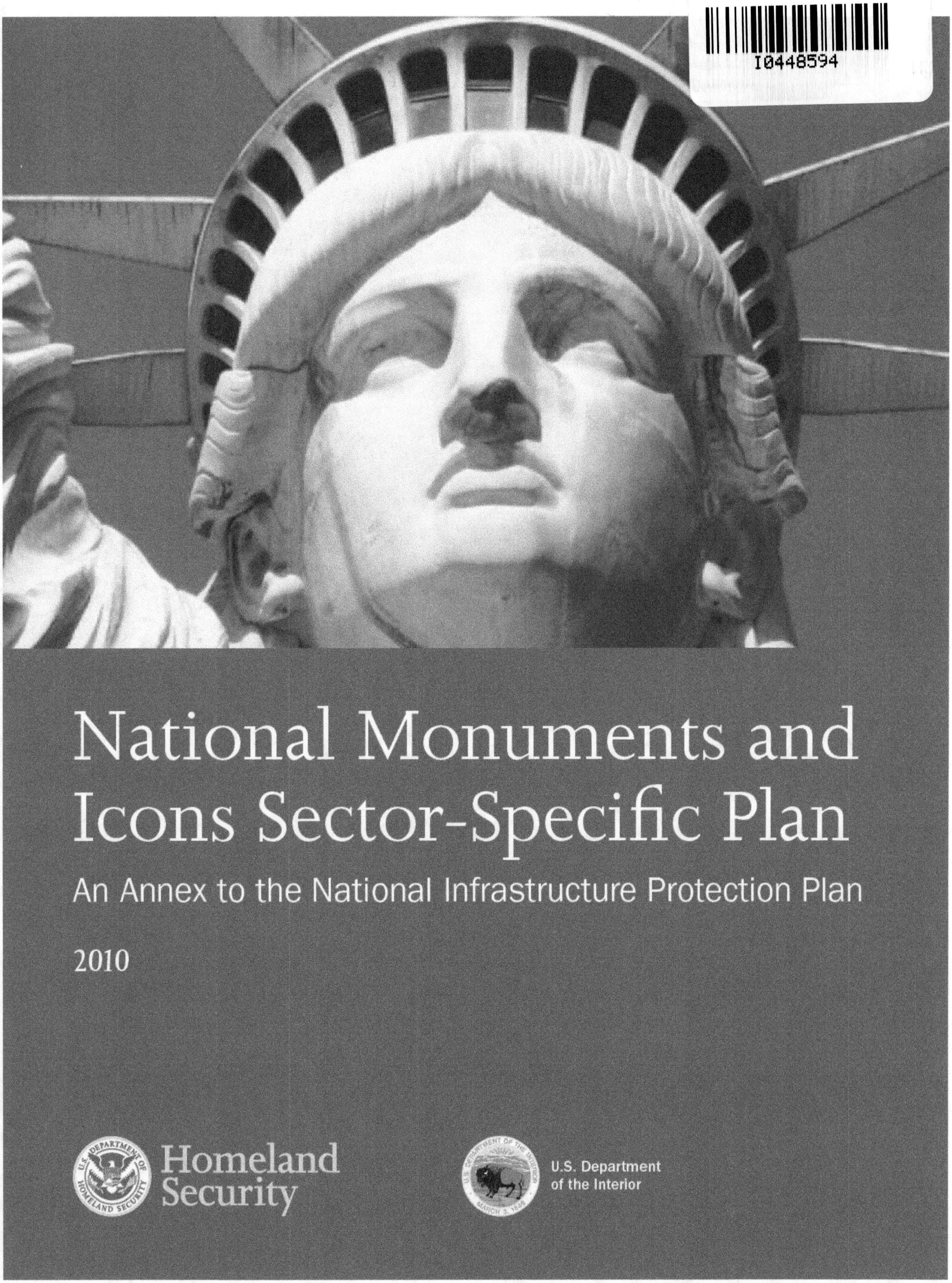

National Monuments and Icons Sector-Specific Plan

An Annex to the National Infrastructure Protection Plan

2010

Preface

The National Infrastructure Protection Plan (NIPP) provides the unifying structure for the integration of critical infrastructure and key resources (CIKR) protection efforts as part of a coordinated national program. The NIPP provides the overarching framework for integrating protective programs and activities that are underway in the various sectors, as well as new and developing CIKR protection efforts. The NIPP includes 18 Sector-Specific Plans (SSPs) that detail the application of the overall risk management framework for each specific sector.

The National Monuments and Icons (NMI) SSP describes a collaborative effort among the various Federal Government agencies that have equities within the NMI Sector and will result in the prioritization of protection initiatives and recommended investments within the NMI Sector as a whole. This prioritization ensures that resources are applied where they contribute the most to risk mitigation by lessening vulnerabilities, deterring threats, and minimizing the consequences of terrorist attacks and other natural and manmade hazards.

This 2010 release of the NMI SSP reflects the maturation of the partnership and the progress of the sector programs first outlined in the 2007 SSP. Examples of sector accomplishments since the publication of the 2007 SSP include:

- The Department of the Interior (DOI) conducted a comprehensive study of the psychosocial impacts of a terrorist attack on an NMI asset, through the Homeland Security Institute in support of U.S. Department of Homeland Security (DHS) Science and Technology Directorate.

- The sector consolidated oversight responsibilities for NMI assets on the National Mall, as well as at the Statue of Liberty, under one senior security manager.

- The sector commissioned a comprehensive risk assessment to determine the likely chemical, biological, and radiological threats that may be used directly against Smithsonian facilities on the National Mall or nearby high-profile facilities.

- DOI opened a new operations center capable of providing situational awareness and decisionmaking support to senior leaders during all-hazard emergencies on a 24-hour basis.

The NMI Sector is committed to ensuring that the symbols of our Nation remain protected and intact for future generations. Because access to monuments and icons is a hallmark of life in a free and open society, the sector will strive for an appropriate balance between security, public access, and aesthetics. The sector will promote protective measures to dissuade adversaries from affecting the national psyche by damaging or destroying these important symbols.

DOI coordinates with our sector partners for updates on an annual basis. In addition, sector partners are requested to submit to DOI (as the NMI Sector-Specific Agency) any updates and/or significant changes to the asset profile or security posture as soon as possible (e.g., addition of a new visitors' center). This new information would then be incorporated into the Infrastructure Data Warehouse. DOI continues to work closely with DHS to ensure that the information is protected and to develop sharing mechanisms to facilitate accessibility to sector partners.

The NMI SSP represents the goals established by the NMI Sector to facilitate the incorporation of all-hazards protective measures to improve awareness, protection, response, and recovery. The sector's goals are driven by a desire to reduce risk to critical assets within the NMI Sector and to promote the continued use and enjoyment of these infrastructure. The sector is committed to supporting risk mitigation activities, for example:

- Protective System Assessments: assessments performed by the respective monuments and icons using the assessment methodology outlined in the SSP to determine whether their protective systems are updated and operating at maximum capability.

- Shared Training, Best Practices, and Intelligence Reporting: Government Coordinating Council (GCC) and sector partners share training opportunities, protective best practices, and intelligence reporting through established portals (i.e., the Homeland Security Information Network)

Each year, the NMI Sector CIKR Protection Annual Report will provide updates on the sector's efforts to identify, prioritize, and coordinate the protection of its critical infrastructure. The Sector Annual Report provides the current priorities of the sector as well as the progress made during the past year in following the plans and strategies set out in the NMI SSP.

The departments and agencies that constitute the NMI GCC commit to:

- Support the NMI SSP concepts and processes, and carry out their assigned functional responsibilities regarding the protection of the NMI CIKR as described herein;

- Work with DOI (the NMI Sector-Specific Agency) and the Secretary of Homeland Security, as appropriate and consistent with their own agency-specific authorities, resources, and programs, to coordinate funding and implementation of programs that enhance NMI CIKR protection;

- Cooperate and coordinate with DOI and the Secretary of Homeland Security, in accordance with guidance provided in Homeland Security Presidential Directive 7, as appropriate and consistent with their respective agency-specific authorities, to facilitate NMI CIKR protection;

- Develop or modify existing interagency and agency specific CIKR plans, as appropriate, to facilitate compliance with the NMI SSP;

- Develop and maintain partnerships for CIKR protection with appropriate State, regional, local, tribal, territorial, and international entities, the private sector, and nongovernmental organizations; and

- Protect critical infrastructure information according to the Protected Critical Infrastructure Information program or other appropriate guidelines, and share CIKR protection-related information, as appropriate and consistent with their own agency-specific authorities and the process described herein.

Kim A. Thorsen

Deputy Assistant Secretary – Law Enforcement,
Security and Emergency Management
U.S. Department of the Interior

Todd M. Keil

Assistant Secretary for Infrastructure Protection
U.S. Department of Homeland Security

Table of Contents

List of Figures

List of Tables

Executive Summary

The National Monuments and Icons (NMI) Sector-Specific Plan (SSP) was created to complement the National Infrastructure Protection Plan (NIPP) in improving protection of the NMI Sector in an all-hazard environment. The NMI SSP promotes a collaborative partnership at all levels of government to foster the cooperation necessary to improve the protection of NMI critical infrastructure and key resources (CIKR). The NMI SSP is a pathway to identify and prioritize assets, assess risk, implement protective programs, and measure the effectiveness of protective programs. This document represents the collaborative efforts of our sector partners, all dedicated to the protection and resilience of CIKR assets as it relates to all hazards within the NMI Sector.

1. Sector Profile and Goals

The NMI Sector encompasses a diverse array of assets located throughout the United States. Many of these NMI assets are listed in either the National Register of Historic Places or the List of National Historic Landmarks.

NMI Sector assets share the following common characteristics:

- A monument, physical structure, or object;
- Recognized both nationally and internationally as representing the Nation's heritage, traditions, and/or values or for their national, cultural, religious, historical, or political significance; or
- Serve the primary purpose of memorializing or representing significant aspects of the Nation's heritage, traditions, or values and as points of interest for visitors and educational activities. They generally do not have a purpose or function that fits under the responsibility of another sector.

NMI Sector assets are essentially physical structures and include the operational staff and visitors who may be impacted by an all-hazard incident. The sector has no infrastructure located outside of the United States and there are no critical foreign dependencies related to the sector. NMI Sector assets do not include famous people or technology applications, and there are minimal cyber and telecommunications issues associated with this sector due to the nature of the assets.

The NMI Sector is committed to ensuring that the symbols of our Nation remain protected and intact for future generations. Because access to monuments and icons is a hallmark of life in a free and open society, the sector will strive for an appropriate balance between security, public access, and aesthetics. The sector will promote protective measures to dissuade adversaries from affecting the national psyche by damaging or destroying these important symbols.

The NMI SSP represents the goals established by the NMI Sector to facilitate the incorporation of all-hazards protective measures to improve awareness, protection, response, and recovery. The sector's goals are driven by a desire to reduce risk to critical assets within the NMI Sector and to promote the continued use and enjoyment of these infrastructures.

The goals of the NMI Sector are as follows:

Goal 1: Continue to review sector criteria to ensure a clear definition of NMI assets.

Goal 2: Delineate and define roles and responsibilities for sector partners.

Goal 3: Continue to encourage sector partners to perform or update risk assessments at NMI Sector assets.

Goal 4: Maintain rapid and robust communications between intelligence and law enforcement agencies and Government Coordinating Council (GCC) partners that operate sector assets.

Goal 5: Maintain seamless coordination among GCC partners that operate sector assets.

Goal 6: Maintain cross-sector coordination with regard to NMI assets whose primary protective responsibility resides in another sector.

Goal 7: Integrate robust security, technology, and practices contingent on agency mission priorities and available resources while preserving the appearance and accessibility of NMI Sector assets.

Goal 8: Review and update security programs to adjust to seasonal and event-specific challenges.

Goal 9: Continue to protect against insider threats.

Goal 10: Update contingency response programs.

2. Identifying Assets, Systems, and Networks

The identification of assets, systems, and networks is necessary to define the NMI Sector and to develop an inventory of CIKR that can be further analyzed with respect to vulnerabilities and the protective actions required to achieve the goals set forth in chapter 1.

The process for identifying and defining new sector assets, systems, and networks continues to be a collaborative effort between the Department of the Interior (DOI), the Department of Homeland Security (DHS), and our GCC partners. DOI continues to work closely with DHS in establishing relationships with the private sector to ensure maximum information exchange within and outside the Federal Government.

3. Assess Risk

The NIPP affirms that risk assessments are essential to the appropriate distribution of the limited funds allocated for infrastructure protection. There is no overarching regulatory authority within the NMI Sector that mandates risk assessments. However, all of the current assets are operated by the Federal Government and are covered by internal requirements mandating risk assessments.

The initial step in the risk assessment process is the characterization of the sector assets and consists of the following two elements:

- A ranking system based on the uniqueness of the asset and its significance as a national symbol; and

- Consequence categories encompassing DHS SSP guidance.

The remaining steps in the process utilize the DHS SSP guidance regarding criteria for consequence, vulnerability, and risk and result in a numerical ranking based on a postulated worst-case scenario.

4. Prioritize Infrastructure

Prioritization for CIKR is used to focus planning, foster coordination, and support the effective allocation of resources as well as for incident management. Resources are applied where they contribute most to the mitigation of identified risks contingent on agency mission priorities.

NMI Sector assets designated have been subjected to the NMI risk assessment methodology to develop a numerical score based on the vulnerabilities associated with each facility. DOI has conducted the assessment for those assets it operates and has encouraged our GCC partners to conduct assessments at their facilities.

5. Develop and Implement Protective Programs and Resilience Strategies

Protective programs involve measures designed to prevent, detect, deter, and mitigate the threat; reduce vulnerability to an all-hazards incident; minimize consequences; and enable timely, efficient response and restoration in a post-event situation.

NMI Sector partners and asset-specific law enforcement have developed and implemented protective programs on an accelerated basis since the terrorist attacks on September 11, 2001. A mix of new regulations, congressional mandates, actual and perceived threat information, and vulnerabilities has driven these programs.

NMI partners have used a methodical, disciplined approach to match limited resources with sector assets and to share validated protective measures across the security spectrum. The participation of sector partners in sharing best practices is paramount to ensuring the highest level of protection for NMI assets.

6. Measure Effectiveness

Objectives and metrics have been developed to measure the progress of the protection efforts. By measuring the effectiveness of the protective programs and actions, the NMI Sector continually improves CIKR mitigation actions at the sector level and improves the overall performance at the national level.

7. CIKR Protection Research and Development

Research and development (R&D) is one of the key tools the sector uses to improve knowledge pertaining to threats, vulnerabilities, consequences, and subsequent risks associated with sector assets when subject to all-hazards incidents.

DOI, as the NMI Sector-Specific Agency (SSA), liaises with the DHS Science and Technology Directorate and the Executive Office of the President's Office of Science and Technology Policy on a periodic basis to identify current R&D initiatives that have applicability to the sector. DOI shares this information with our sector partners to gather input relative to those initiatives of most value to the sector.

8. Managing and Coordinating SSA Responsibilities

The SSA continues to capitalize on the cooperation and coordination that exists among our sector partners to accomplish the numerous tasks assigned to the SSA and ensures that the sector meets its goals and objectives.

Introduction

Protecting the critical infrastructure and key resources (CIKR) of the United States is essential to the Nation's security, economic vitality, and way of life. CIKR includes the assets, systems, and networks that provide vital services to the Nation. Terrorist attacks on CIKR and other natural and manmade hazards could significantly disrupt the functioning of government and business alike and produce cascading effects far beyond the affected CIKR sector and physical location of the incident. Direct attacks could result in large-scale human casualties, property destruction, and economic damage, and also profoundly damage national prestige, morale, and confidence. Terrorist attacks that use components of the Nation's CIKR as weapons of mass destruction[1] could have even more devastating physical, psychological, and economic consequences.

The protection of CIKR is, therefore, an essential component of the homeland security mission to make America safer, more secure, and more resilient from terrorist attacks and all-hazards incidents. Protection includes actions to guard or shield CIKR assets, systems, networks, or their interconnecting links from exposure, injury, destruction, incapacitation, or exploitation. In the context of the National Infrastructure Protection Plan (NIPP), this includes actions to deter, mitigate, or neutralize the threat, vulnerability, or consequences associated with a terrorist attack or all-hazards incident. Protection can include a wide range of activities, including hardening facilities, building resilience and redundancy, incorporating hazard resistance into initial facility design, initiating active or passive countermeasures, installing security systems, promoting personal surety programs, and implementing cybersecurity measures. The NIPP provides the framework for the unprecedented cooperation that is needed to develop, implement, and maintain a coordinated national effort that brings together government at all levels, the private sector, and international organizations and allies.

The NIPP and its complementary Sector-Specific Plans (SSPs) provide a consistent, unifying structure for integrating both existing and future CIKR protection efforts. It also provides the core processes and mechanisms to enable government and private sector partners to work together to implement CIKR protection initiatives. Homeland Security Presidential Directive 7 (HSPD-7) and the NIPP outline 18 CIKR sectors in recognition that each sector possesses unique characteristics and operating methods. The Department of the Interior (DOI), as the Sector-Specific Agency (SSA) for the National Monuments and Icons (NMI) Sector, is responsible for developing and updating the SSP for this sector.

The purpose of the SSP is to detail the application of the NIPP risk management framework to each of the 18 sectors. The SSPs were developed and updated by the designated Federal SSAs in coordination with relevant sector partners. The SSP for each sector should align with the processes established in the NIPP, most notably the risk management framework. Each SSP should

---

[1] (1) Any explosive, incendiary, or poison gas (i) bomb, (ii) grenade, (iii) rocket having a propellant charge of more than 4 ounces, (iv) missile having an explosive or incendiary charge of more than one-quarter ounce, or (v) mine or (vi) similar device; (2) any weapon that is designed or intended to cause death or serious bodily injury through the release, dissemination, or impact of toxic or poisonous chemicals or their precursors; (3) any weapon involving a disease organism; or (4) any weapon that is designed to release radiation or radioactivity at a level dangerous to human life (18 U.S.C. 2332a).

support the planning assumptions outlined in the NIPP, as well as sector-specific planning assumptions that are relevant to protection of that sector's CIKR. This document presents the SSP for the NMI Sector.

The National Strategy for the Physical Protection of Critical Infrastructures and Key Assets, published in February 2003, defined the NMI Sector as the "diverse array of national monuments, symbols, and icons that represent our Nation's heritage, traditions and values, and political power. They include a wide variety of sites and structures such as prominent historical attractions, monuments, cultural icons, and centers of government and commerce." In addition, the U.S. Department of Homeland Security's (DHS) 2004 guidance for developing SSPs states that "icons can be considered to include any structure, system, or resource that has cultural, historic, psychological, or political significance at the local, regional, or national level if compromised or destroyed." Terrorists perceive NMI assets as internationally recognized symbols of American power, culture, and democratic tradition. Terrorist targets most frequently represent a confluence of these factors and the pragmatic concerns of loss of life, continuous live media coverage, strategic economic impact, and potential for infrastructure interdependency.

A ranking system will determine if a monument or icon is a National Critical, National Significant, Regional Critical, or Local Significant NMI asset. Assets included in this sector are monuments and icons ranked as National Critical, such as those located in the Nation's capital as well as others such as the Statue of Liberty, Independence Hall, the Liberty Bell, and Mount Rushmore National Monument. This sector also encompasses buildings, institutions, and landmark architectural structures. All of the assets within the sector are operated by the Federal Government.

Assets with iconic value that best fit in one of the other sectors, such as Dams, Commercial Facilities, and Government Facilities, have not been included within the NMI SSP. However, DOI has supported other SSAs to ensure appropriate risk ranking and implementation of protective programs for those assets.

The NMI SSP provides the impetus for collaboration with stakeholders who share responsibility for protecting the Nation's NMI assets.

A number of key limitations affect the environment in which DOI, as the SSA, strives to develop programs to protect NMI assets:

- First, except for monuments and iconic sites operated by the National Park Service (NPS), DOI has no existing or historical regulatory or oversight relationships with any entities within the sector.

- Second, changes designed to enhance security may face severe limitations because of the historic nature of many assets and their surrounding areas. Examples include the icons on the National Mall in Washington, D.C. The NPS must submit proposed security enhancements to the National Capitol Planning Commission and the Fine Arts Commission for review and approval. Although this is a critical process that maintains the visual and historical integrity of the assets and surrounding areas, the review frequently results in disapproval or modification of the proposed security enhancements.

- Finally, by their very nature, most assets within this sector are designed and managed as open sites that welcome visitors from this country and from around the world. These sites are intended to be visited and enjoyed, to provide areas for learning and contemplation, and to connect current and future generations to historical events and locations in the Nation's past. Maintaining the open design of these sites, while addressing the need to improve protection, leads to conflicting considerations, both internally and externally with regard to the level and type of protective measures to be used.

1. Sector Profile and Goals

1.1 Sector Profile

The NMI Sector encompasses a diverse array of assets, systems, and networks located throughout the United States. Many of the assets are listed in either the National Register of Historic Places or the List of National Historic Landmarks.

NMI Sector assets share the following common characteristics:

- A monument, physical structure, or object;
- Recognized both nationally and internationally as representing the Nation's heritage, traditions, and/or values or for their national, cultural, religious, historical, or political significance; or
- Serve the primary purpose of memorializing or representing significant aspects of the Nation's heritage, traditions, or values and as points of interest for visitors and educational activities. They generally do not have a purpose or function that fits under the responsibility of another sector.

Some physical structures that could be considered monuments or icons (e.g., Golden Gate Bridge, Sears Tower, Hoover Dam, and the U.S. Capitol) have been determined to be more appropriately assigned to other sectors, such as Defense Industrial Base, Transportation Systems, Commercial Facilities, Dams, or Government Facilities, based on their primary purposes. This sector assignment is intended to ensure a better level of security based on application of more appropriate protective measures and programs. DOI, as the SSA, confers with other SSAs and is represented on their Government Coordinating Councils (GCCs).

NMI assets are primarily physical structures. Included as part of each asset are the operational staff and visitors that may be impacted by a terrorist attack or all-hazards incident. Sector assets do not include famous people or technology applications, although they may contain holdings of significant importance to the Nation's history. There are negligible cyber and telecommunications issues associated with this sector due to the nature of the assets. However, for any future initiatives, the Bureau Chief Information Officer (CIO) or his delegate is a member of the IT GCC and is responsible for providing oversight for the cyber-based information systems located at DOI-operated assets; this responsibility may be delegated to the system owner. In conjunction with the system security manager, the system owner is responsible for the overall security of the IT system, including certification and accreditation, categorization of systems as general support systems or major applications, and preparation of system security plans. DOI policy applies to all IT systems that process Sensitive But Unclassified (SBU) data (all unclassified DOI systems are considered SBU).

Certain national holidays, such as the Fourth of July, Memorial Day, and Labor Day, represent an especially important factor for this sector, when visitation at selected NMI assets is particularly high. Special date events are discussed with respect to the development of protective programs in chapter 5.

Although a diverse array of NMI assets are scattered across the United States and its Territories, this SSP focuses primarily on identifying, prioritizing, assessing, and protecting NMI assets designated as National Critical.

1.2 Sector Partners

Recognizing that each infrastructure sector possesses its own unique characteristics and operating models, HSPD-7 has designated SSAs in each critical infrastructure sector that have primary responsibility for leading protective program efforts for the assets in that sector. In accordance with the guidance provided by HSPD-7, as the SSA for NMI assets, DOI continues to perform the following:

- Work with the operators of NMI assets designated as National Critical to identify, prioritize, and coordinate protection efforts to prevent, deter, and mitigate the effects of a terrorist attack or all-hazards incident;

- Collaborate with non-NMI Sector Federal departments and agencies on protective issues;

- Conduct vulnerability assessments of DOI-operated assets and encourage operators of non-DOI-owned assets to conduct similar reviews; and

- Encourage adoption of risk management strategies to protect against and mitigate the effects of a terrorist attack or all-hazards incident against CIKR.

1.2.1 Sector-Specific Agency

Department of the Interior. DOI was created by an act of Congress in 1849 to manage public lands. DOI has long been involved in the protection of NMI assets, such as the Washington Monument and the Statue of Liberty. DOI manages the third largest Federal law enforcement force, with approximately 4,400 commissioned law enforcement personnel spread among the Bureau of Indian Affairs, Bureau of Land Management, Bureau of Reclamation (BOR), Fish and Wildlife Service, and the NPS. In addition, approximately 1,300 tribal and contract law enforcement personnel serve on Indian country lands. DOI is responsible for the safety and security of 70,000 employees and 200,000 volunteers, 1.3 million daily visitors, and more than 507 million acres of public lands that include historic or nationally significant sites as well as dams and reservoirs. Over the last several years, BOR has completed security vulnerability assessments (VAs) of its dams, power plants, and canals in the 17 Western States. In addition, DOI assists in providing security for oil and gas production and transmission facilities on Federal and Indian trust lands, including 4,000 offshore oil and gas production facilities, 22,000 miles of active pipelines, and 35,000 petroleum workers in the Gulf of Mexico.

All cyber systems within NMI Sector assets are required to comply with regulations outlined in the Federal Information Security Management Act (FISMA) and must be certified and accredited. Each must follow the standardized certification and accreditation (C&A) process that is based on the National Institute of Standards and Technology's (NIST) Special Publication 800 series. Additional requirements of the C&A process involve methods to identify and prioritize cyber systems, discover and remediate vulnerabilities, and test protective measures.

DOI is an active partner in multiagency task forces that facilitate the sharing of information, developing security protocols, and identifying protective measures designed to prevent and respond to real and potential terrorist attacks. In the wake of 9/11, DOI's efforts were intensified to match the increased threat environment.

1.2.2 Federal Departments and Agencies

Smithsonian Institution (SI). In 1826, James Smithson, a British scientist, drew up his last will and testament, naming his nephew as beneficiary. Smithson stipulated that if his nephew should die without heirs (as he would in 1835), the estate should go "to the United States of America, to found at Washington, under the name of the Smithsonian Institution, an establishment for the increase and diffusion of knowledge among men."

Smithson died in 1829, and six years later, President Andrew Jackson announced the bequest to the U.S. Congress. On July 1, 1836, Congress accepted the legacy bequeathed to the Nation and pledged the faith of the United States to the charitable trust. An act of Congress signed by President James K. Polk on August 10, 1846, established the SI as a trust to be administered by a board of regents and a secretary of the Smithsonian.

SI's Office of Protection Services (OPS) provides security services and operates programs for security management and criminal investigations at SI facilities on and near the National Mall in Washington, D.C., in New York City, and in Panama. OPS provides technical assistance and advisory services to SI bureaus, offices, and facilities. It serves SI employees and volunteers, and more than 25 million visitors each year. The United States Code (40 U.S.C. 6301-6307) provided OPS the authority to police the buildings and grounds of the SI.

National Archives and Records Administration (NARA). The mission of NARA is to take cost-effective steps to protect the holdings of our archival and records center in an appropriate space, ensure protection and preservation of records, and expand storage capacities to meet growing demands. NARA's authority is codified principally under 44 U.S.C. Chapters 21-33.

NARA also ensures that the President, Congress, the courts, public servants, and citizens continue to have access to the essential evidence that documents the rights of American citizens and the actions of Federal officials, promotes civic education, and facilitates a historical understanding of our national experience. NARA sets the minimum structural, environmental, property, and life-safety standards that a records storage facility must meet in order to be used to safeguard and preserve the records of our government and ensure that the people can discover, use, and learn from this documentary heritage.

Department of Homeland Security (DHS). As set forth in HSPD-7, DHS is responsible for coordinating the overall national effort to enhance protection of the CIKR of the United States. DHS is also responsible for establishing uniform policies, approaches, guidelines, and methodologies for integrating Federal infrastructure protection and risk management activities within and across sectors along with metrics and criteria for related programs and activities. DHS has overseen the development of the NIPP and is responsible for providing guidance for SSP approaches and methodologies. During implementation, DHS has led, integrated, and coordinated efforts among Federal departments and agencies, State and local governments, and the private sector.

Specifically within DHS, the Office of Infrastructure Protection (IP) provides oversight of the NMI SSP and the Science and Technology Directorate (S&T) provides support. DHS has coordinated relationships with the private sector to ensure maximum information exchange within and outside the Federal Government.

The mutual collaboration and agreement between DOI and DHS is critical regarding overlaps and interdependencies where the type and character of the NMI asset falls primarily into a CIKR sector for which DHS is the SSA. DOI routinely confers with DHS and the other SSAs to clearly identify these overlaps and interdependencies and has reached consensus on responsibilities for these NMI assets within the respective sectors. For example:

- Transportation Systems Sector with respect to bridges (e.g., Golden Gate Bridge);
- Dams Sector (e.g., Hoover Dam);
- Government Facilities Sector (e.g., U.S. Capitol); and
- Commercial Facilities Sector (e.g., Empire State Building).

DOI routinely confers with DHS to clearly delineate lead and support roles and responsibilities. In its support role, DOI provides assistance to DHS with respect to the overall protection of these assets.

Department of Defense (DoD). DoD is responsible for providing the military forces needed to deter war and protect the security of our country. Each military department (the Department of the Navy includes naval aviation and the United States Marine Corps) is separately organized under its own Secretary and functions under the authority, direction, and control of the Secretary of Defense. The Navy currently operates approximately 285 commissioned ships, including the USS Constitution which is included in the NMI Sector.

Office of Science and Technology Policy (OSTP). The OSTP has a broad mandate to advise the President and others within the Executive Office of the President on the effects of science and technology on domestic and international affairs. The office is also authorized to lead an interagency effort to develop and implement sound science and technology policies and budgets and to work with the private sector, State and local governments, the science and higher education communities, and other nations toward this end.

The OSTP has supported DOI in developing the NMI SSP and has been included as appropriate in policy development, protective program plans and related technology development, operational discussions, and coordination meetings. DOI, as the SSA, coordinates with the OSTP to take advantage of available support resources.

Other Federal Agencies. Other Federal agencies operate buildings, structures, and systems that could be categorized as NMI assets. The assets under the responsibility of these Federal agencies would be included as CIKR under the Government Facilities, Defense Industrial Base, or Transportation Systems Sectors. DOI, as the SSA, works closely with DHS and other Federal agencies to clearly delineate lead and support roles and responsibilities.

1.2.3 State, Local, Tribal, and Territorial Governments

Relationships With State, Local, Tribal, and Territorial Governments

State, local, tribal, and territorial authorities typically own or regulate regional and local NMI assets. DOI, as the SSA for the NMI Sector, will work closely with DHS in establishing relationships with State Offices of Homeland Security to ensure maximum information exchange within and outside the Federal Government. These State offices, in conjunction with DHS, will develop a close working relationship with other State and local agencies responsible for NMI assets as a major part of outreach efforts. As part of the asset identification process, DOI will engage DHS and the State Offices of Homeland Security to gather information from agencies and organizations within each State.

Generally, if monuments and icons under State, local, or tribal control are considered nationally significant NMI assets, they would be included within the Commercial Facilities or Government Facilities Sectors. DHS is the lead SSA for these two sectors. DOI will work with DHS to delineate lead and support roles and responsibilities.

1.2.4 Private Sector

Private sector firms function as an adjunct to but not a replacement for public law enforcement by helping to reduce and prevent crime. They protect individuals, property, and proprietary information, and provide protection for banks, hospitals, research and development (R&D) centers, manufacturing facilities, defense and aerospace contractors, high technology businesses, nuclear power plants, chemical companies, oil and gas refineries, airports, communication facilities and operations, office complexes, schools, private universities, residential properties, apartment complexes, gated communities, museums, sporting events, and theme parks. Private sector security and law enforcement entities derive their authority from State, regional, and local laws in effect for their jurisdictions or areas of responsibility. Many assets within the NMI Sector utilize private security guards under contract, both armed and unarmed, as their sole security force or to supplement their law enforcement and security staffs.

Relationships with private sector facilities currently exist but are limited. DOI, as the SSA for the NMI Sector, relies on the State, Local, Tribal, and Territorial Government Coordinating Council as well as the Government Facilities Sector to ensure information exchange with organizations occurs outside the Federal Government.

1.3 Sector Goals and Objectives

Sector goals state the comprehensive protective posture that our sector partners are working together to achieve and will help lead to a steady state of protection.

These goals were developed using the full spectrum of protective and resilience activities (i.e., awareness, prevention, protection, response, and recovery). These five areas correspond to the five goals established in the DHS Strategic Plan.

Awareness

Threats

Following the September 11th attacks, DOI initiated a review of security policies at hundreds of DOI-operated assets meeting the criteria as monuments or icons. Conscious of the need to expedite implementation of enhanced security measures, DOI quickly initiated efforts to identify assets at risk of terrorist attack. In doing so, the Department focused specific attention on those assets commonly recognized within the national or international community as being symbolic or iconic of the United States. At the conclusion of this effort, DOI identified assets warranting special protective measures. These assets came to be referred to as National Monuments and Icons. Since completing the initial identification effort, DOI has reevaluated this assessment to ensure that each asset continues to be appropriately designated.

Vulnerability

The priority assets have been subjected to VAs that rank each asset based on the nature of the threat as well as the consequences of a terrorist attack or all-hazards incident.

Impacts

Unlike other assets that have numerous interdependencies, NMI assets are basically stand-alone assets. The loss of or damage to an NMI asset generally will not have a cascading effect on other assets within the NMI Sector, or other sectors, such as Energy, Transportation Systems, Agriculture and Food, and so on. Damage to an NMI asset could undoubtedly result in a drastic increase in security, and possible closure, of other NMI assets. Also, the economic impact of an attack may significantly affect the local and national tourism industry. However, the greatest potential impact will be on the national psyche. An attack on an NMI asset could result in significant loss of life and intense media coverage with visual reminders of the death and destruction. It could also reduce public confidence in our Nation's ability to protect its citizens and resources against a terrorist attack or respond to an all-hazards incident.

Prevention

Detection

The ability of intelligence agencies to detect potential terrorist attacks has been enhanced significantly in recent years. A critical component of any attack is prior surveillance of the target. This is also one of the points where our adversaries are the most vulnerable. A robust and effective countersurveillance program is critical to detecting the pre-attack indicators.

Countersurveillance relies heavily on the law enforcement and security staffs at or near an asset. An often overlooked component of countersurveillance is the observations of non-law enforcement personnel at the site, such as maintenance workers, interpretive staff, and volunteers. These individuals are thoroughly familiar with the area and may be cognizant of anything or anyone who seems out of place. By reporting their observations to law enforcement, they have a major impact on deterring an attack.

Deterrence

The results of a VA will demonstrate where each asset is most susceptible to an attack. Combined with a risk assessment, the VA will determine the measures that must be taken for each asset, and in what order, to reduce the risk of an attack to an acceptable level.

Depending on the assessments, as well as the particular situation at each site, the increased protective measures are as simple as restricting parking adjacent to the facility or as complex as building an effective vehicle deterrence system. In some cases small, low-cost changes can have a significant impact on deterring potential attacks.

We have found that in many instances, implementing certain protective measures at the asset is not feasible due to costs or other influences involving the historic footprint of the site. In these cases, the mitigation of a potential attack receives added emphasis.

Mitigation

Because of the accessible nature of this sector's assets, many of the detection and deterrence measures used in other sectors are not available or are not acceptable to asset operators, oversight committees, or the public. For those threats that cannot be deterred, an effective mitigation plan must be established. In many cases, this means a close coordination with local emergency services agencies to ensure a quick and effective response to any incident.

Protection

The concept of protection differs within the NMI Sector as compared to other sectors due to the accessibility of most sites. Whereas other sectors can institute protective measures that restrict access to the asset, the NMI Sector must use protective measures that do not unnecessarily impede access and are not overly visible.

In the post-September 11th era, citizens are more accepting of protective measures but only to a point. For some of the sector's high-profile targets, such as the Statue of Liberty and the Washington Monument, the use of magnetometers and x-ray machines to screen visitors has been successfully implemented. In other more open sites, such as the Lincoln Memorial and Mount Rushmore National Monument, visitors are not screened.

Vehicle-borne improvised explosive devices (VBIED) are an area of concern at many sites. Some sites have little or no standoff distance from major roadways and are extremely vulnerable to VBIEDs, highlighting the need for innovative approaches to reducing this vulnerability.

The release of a chemical, biological, radiological, or nuclear agent is also a concern at many sites. Some sites have detection sensors in place while others are connected to area-wide networks, but many have no detection equipment in place. The cost of responding to false alarms is problematic. In many instances, the expense needed to adequately safeguard against these types of attacks does not justify the additional margin of protection.

Response

In the case of threats that NMI assets cannot adequately protect against, the capability must be in place to mitigate the effects of a potential attack.

A key issue related to several potential attack scenarios is the ability to respond quickly with onsite security personnel to prevent the attack or minimize the effects. For those sites where onsite security is adequate for general activities but insufficient to deal with an attack, coordination with local first responders to quickly supplement the onsite resources has been established.

Recovery

Most NMI assets do not have interdependencies with other sectors and are not a critical component to the operation of other sectors. The time needed to restore the sites following an attack or all-hazards incident is not as critical as it is in other sectors. In some cases, the best course of action should an attack or all-hazards incident destroy an asset would be not to rebuild the asset. This makes protection more relevant than resilience for the sector.

The successful efforts taken to meet the goals and objectives in the sector, while addressing these five protective activities, have assisted the NMI Sector in developing a long-term security plan.

1.3.1 Elements and Characteristics of Sector Goals and Objectives

Vision Statement for the NMI Sector

The NMI Sector is committed to ensuring that the symbols of our Nation remain protected and intact for future generations. In the course of protecting our landmarks, the sector will ensure that staff and visitors are protected from harm. Because citizen access to these monuments and icons is a hallmark of life in a free and open society, the sector will strive for an appropriate balance between security, ease of public access, and aesthetics. However, the sector's ultimate goal is to provide the appropriate security posture that will discourage America's adversaries from choosing our NMI assets as opportune targets.

The goals of the NMI Sector are as follows:

Goal 1: Continue to review sector criteria to ensure a clear definition of NMI assets.

Goal 2: Delineate and define roles and responsibilities for sector partners.

Goal 3: Continue to encourage sector partners to perform or update risk assessments at NMI Sector assets.

Goal 4: Maintain rapid and robust communications between intelligence and law enforcement agencies and Government Coordinating Council (GCC) partners that operate sector assets.

Goal 5: Maintain seamless coordination among GCC partners that operate sector assets.

Goal 6: Maintain cross-sector coordination with regard to NMI assets whose primary protective responsibility resides in another sector.

Goal 7: Integrate robust security, technology, and practices contingent on agency mission priorities and available resources while preserving the appearance and accessibility of NMI Sector assets.

Goal 8: Review and update security programs to adjust to seasonal and event-specific security challenges.

Goal 9: Continue to protect against insider threats.

Goal 10: Update contingency response programs.

1.3.2 Process to Establish Sector Goals

The focus of the NMI Sector has been directed toward effectively securing assets designated through consensus of our sector partners and DHS as National Critical. NMI Sector sites encourage visitation and generally strive to present an open and accessible posture. To further complicate the issue, many assets must obtain approval from advisory or preservation groups before any modifications can be made to the site, whether security related or not.

The types of assets within the sector, and the outside influences on each asset, make it impossible to create one security plan to fit all. Some of these outside influences include the following:

- **Property around an asset belonging to another entity or jurisdiction:** An example of this would be at Independence National Historical Park, where a city street divides Independence Hall and the Liberty Bell Center. The city's decision to keep the roadway open has created security challenges.

- **Location in a remote area:** At Mount Rushmore National Monument, for instance, the nearest available emergency responder in the event of a terrorist attack or all-hazards incident may at times be more than 30 minutes away. As a result, staffing levels have been increased to stabilize an incident until additional resources can arrive.

- **An asset belonging to another agency located on DOI property:** The USS Constitution is located in Boston National Historical Park. The vessel is commissioned as a U.S. Navy warship and is staffed by Navy personnel but open to the public. This creates unique challenges for the NPS and the Navy as they jointly manage and protect the asset.

These challenges have resulted in different security plans being developed at each site. They do, however, have the same basic detection and deterrence methods underlying the plans.

1.4 Value Proposition

All of the assets in the sector are operated by the Federal Government. An impediment to an effective infrastructure protection program is the desire to maintain the accessibility of the assets.

Security officials charged with protecting the asset are faced with justifying proposed protective measures to their agency decision makers, commissions, or boards with architectural oversight authority (e.g., fine arts commissions and regional and local planning commissions), and, to a lesser extent, the visiting public. Therefore, it is imperative that emerging security and protection technology be cost effective and unobtrusive.

In addition, emerging security and protective technology that is cost effective and can act as a force multiplier is desirable. This is a key challenge to be addressed by future technology.

Federally operated assets are self insured; the destruction of the asset will more than likely result in extreme pressure to replace the asset. Rebuilding costs will greatly exceed the cost to adequately protect the asset.

2. Identify Assets, Systems, and Networks

The process of identifying NMI assets continues to be a collaborative effort between DOI, DHS, and the NMI GCC.

2.1 Defining Information Parameters

Figure 2-1 illustrates the process flow for identifying NMI assets.

Figure 2-1: NMI Asset Identification

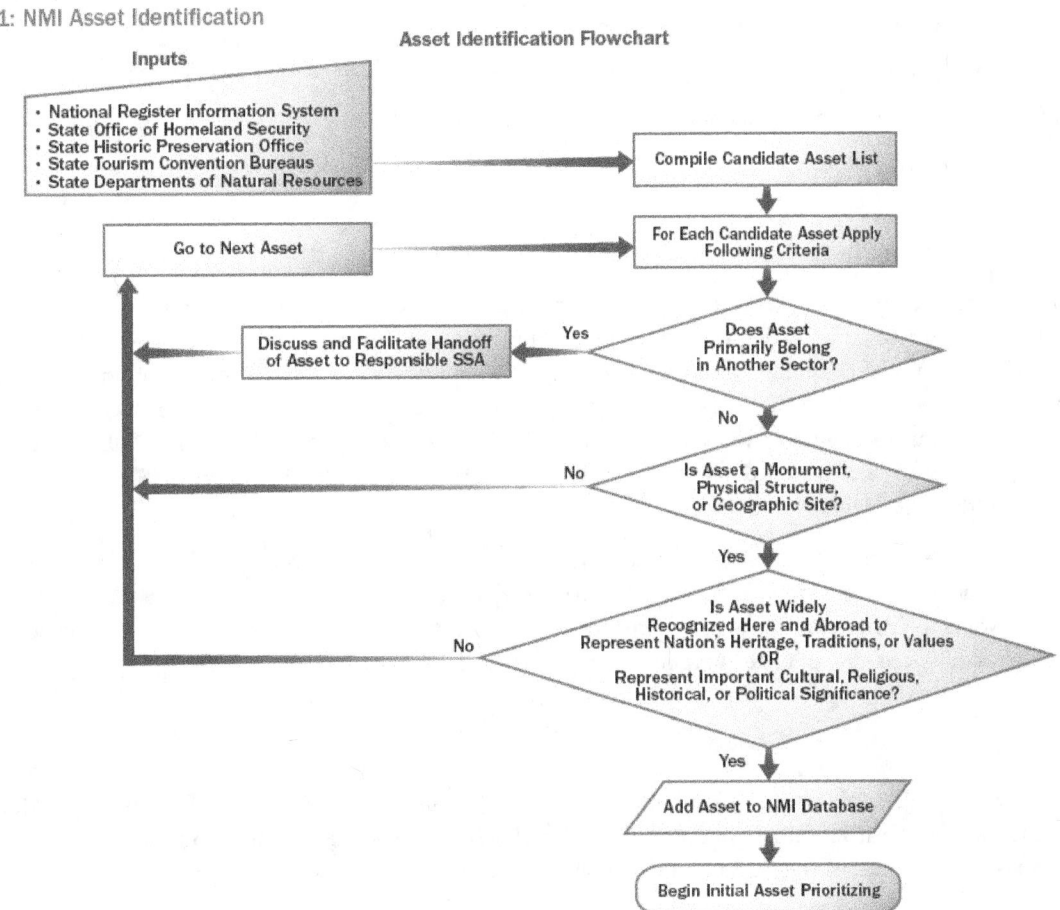

DOI has collaborated with DHS to develop a set of asset characteristics that ensure consistency in data collection across the sector. The taxonomy developed for the NMI Sector breaks down the assets into the following categories:

- National Monument/Icon Structures
  - Buildings
  - Monuments
  - Other Monument/Icon Structures
- National Monument/Icon Geographic Areas
  - Parks
  - Historical Areas
- National Monument/Icon Documents and Objects
  - Historical/Significant Documents
  - Historical/Significant Objects
  - Other National Monuments/Icons

Specific data collected for each of the NMI Sector assets are stored in the Infrastructure Data Warehouse (IDW) and include:

- Asset name and address or general description of location;
- Responsible operator and address;
- Category of asset within the sector (e.g., monument, building, museum, etc.); and
- Purpose and basis for asset's criticality.

2.2 Collecting Infrastructure Information

Some stakeholder information may contain confidential, proprietary, or business-sensitive data. The information is exempt from public disclosure in accordance with the Protected Critical Infrastructure Information (PCII) program, implemented by 6 CFR Part 29. The PCII program requires rigorous safeguarding and handling procedures to prevent unauthorized access to information submitted under the program. This information must be voluntarily submitted directly to DHS and be accompanied by an Express Statement requesting protection under the Critical Infrastructure Information Act of 2002. All information requests to NMI asset stakeholders will be developed in close coordination with DOI legal staff and DHS PCII program representatives to ensure that PCII program requirements are met.

NMI Sector partners have completed an analysis of cyber assets in accordance with DHS National Cyber Security Division (NCSD) guidance. The results of this analysis indicate that the sector's cyber assets are not sufficiently critical that damaging or destroying them would interfere with the continued operation of a sector facility. Cyber assets are used primarily for security and redundant physical systems are in place as backup in the event that a cyber system fails.

2.3 Verifying Infrastructure Information

Additional verification of National Critical NMI information from DOI-owned assets will likely be minimal. For additional assets deemed appropriate for inclusion within this sector, DOI will work through the NMI GCC to verify the data. Depending on the asset and resources available, site visits to selected non-DOI owned assets may be necessary to verify the information.

2.4 Updating Infrastructure Information

DOI coordinates with our sector partners for updates on an annual basis. In addition, sector partners are requested to submit to their SSA any updates and/or significant changes to the asset profile or security posture as soon as possible (e.g., addition of a new visitors' center). This new information would then be incorporated into the IDW. DOI will continue to work closely with DHS to ensure that the information is protected and develop sharing mechanisms to facilitate accessibility to sector partners.

3. Assess Risks

DOI and our sector partners have performed risk assessments for their assets. Several discussions have occurred with DHS concerning normalizing risk assessments to establish a common threat picture across all sectors. The NMI Sector will continue to work closely with DHS in this regard.

3.1 Use of Risk Assessment in the Sector

A terrorist attack or all-hazards incident at an NMI asset could impact national morale and confidence; cause significant loss of life and casualties, political and economic disruption, or environmental damage; and, in some instances, have a negative impact on other CIKR sectors. Due to these potential consequences, the vulnerabilities of our Nation's NMI assets and the threat of an attack or all-hazards incident must be assessed so measures and programs can be implemented to protect these symbols of national culture and heritage.

Because cross-sector impacts of a terrorist attack or an all-hazards incident on an NMI asset would be limited, and because most of the assets are stand-alone entities that are not tied to each other in any way, risk assessments are performed for each specific asset and not as part of a network or system.

No overarching regulatory authority within the sector mandates risk assessments. However, all of the assets are operated by the Federal Government and are covered by internal requirements mandating risk assessments.

In addition, the NIPP requires that the SSAs lead sector-specific risk management programs as part of the overall effort to ensure a steady state of protection within and across the CIKR sectors.

3.2 Screening Infrastructure

The initial step in the risk assessment process is the characterization of the sector assets and comprises the following two elements:

- A ranking system based on the uniqueness of the asset and its significance as a national symbol; and
- Consequence categories encompassing SSP guidance from DHS.

The first step in the risk assessment process is independent of the threat scenario and is a measure of the impact on the national morale and public confidence caused by damage or destruction of a significant monument or icon. The ranking system will determine if a monument or icon is a National Critical, National Significant, Regional Critical, or Local Significant NMI asset.

The concept is defined in table 3-1. For purposes of consistency and standardization, the National Significant, Regional Critical, and Local Significant categories are added for application of the methodology by State, regional, and local authorities. The NMI SSP will assess those assets designated as National Critical.

Other assets will be assessed by the requisite authority, with support as necessary from DHS and DOI.

Table 3-1: Tier Levels

Tier Level	NMI Asset Characteristics	Point Value
National Critical	Assets of unique quality, widely recognized both nationally and internationally to be symbolic of the United States.	
National Significant	Assets generally recognized nationally to be significant symbols of the United States.	
Regional Critical	Assets of unique quality, widely recognized as having significance on a regional level.	
Local Significant	Assets generally recognized as significant on a local level.	

3.3 Assessing Consequences

The second step of the process uses the SSP guidance developed by DHS regarding criteria for consequence categories and results in a numerical ranking based on postulated, worst-case scenarios. The estimates used in the following exhibits are derived from modeling and elicitation of expert opinions. The consequence categories are defined as follows.

- **Loss of Life and/or Casualties:** A measure of the number of individuals (under normal/average visitation) that could be killed or wounded in and around the asset's immediate area;

- **Economic Impact:** A measure of overall dollar-cost impact, including direct and indirect loss of business and tourism revenue, economic impacts on overlapping sectors, costs of emergency response, costs of environmental cleanup, and so on;

- **Length of Outage/Disruption:** A measure of the length of time it would take to resume normal operations;

- **Impact to Other Sectors:** A measure of asset interdependency reflected in a correlated loss of function in other sectors; and

- **Environmental Impact:** A measure of the acreage impacted, including direct and indirect effects on natural resources and wildlife, loss of use due to environmental damage and associated remediation, and so on.

Due to the irreplaceable value of NMI assets and their unique importance to our culture and national heritage, the overall consequence calculation is weighted higher (by a factor of two to one) in the tier-ranking exercise in section 3.2 than the impacts based on the categories outlined in this section: casualties, economic impact, length of outage/disruption, impact to other sectors, and environmental impact. This results in a prioritization based on symbolic value and impact on the public morale and confidence as the prime considerations for the NMI Sector.

Once the impact of the threat scenarios is determined and the tier consequence value is established, the total consequence ranking for each threat scenario as applied to an asset can be calculated. The consequence ranking for each threat scenario is determined by the sum of the individual numerical rankings from each consequence category. The calculation may be expressed in a numerical equation as follows:

$$C_{\text{Attack Scenario Total}} = (2 \times C_{\text{Tier Level}}) + C_{\text{Casualties}} + C_{\text{Economic Impact}} + C_{\text{Length of Outage/Disruption}}$$

$$+ C_{\text{Impact to Other Sectors}} + C_{\text{Environmental Impact}}$$

Each of these consequence categories will include a numerical ranking that assigns the impact of the scenario into bins of consequences. Appropriate technical expertise, specifically DHS/IASD, will be utilized as required during the performance and review of initial consequence assessments for NMI components. See table 3-2 for an example of the consequence value table.

This worst-case consequence assessment provides an initial prioritization of National Critical NMI assets and establishes the basis for the subsequent detailed analysis of consequences.

With relation to cyber, because all of the sector assets are stand-alone and Federal, there is minimal interconnectivity between the assets and there are no common infrastructure partnerships between any of the other 17 sectors. In the event the cyber posture would change within the sector, DOI would partner with DHS/NCSD to obtain technical expertise related to cyber consequences.

Table 3-2: Consequence Values

Atack Scenario	Asset Tier Level	Number of Casualties	Economic Impact	Length of Outage	Impact to Other Sectors	Environ-mental Impact	Total Conse-quence Value
	Tier Level + Casualties + Economic + Outage + Other Sectors + Environmental = Attack Scenario Total						
						Overall Consequence Value for Asset	

3.4 Assessing Vulnerabilities

This section outlines the process of how National Critical NMI assets (including critical information and telecommunications components) will be assessed to identify vulnerabilities to possible terrorist activities or all-hazards events. The section also presents the methodology for determining the overall risk. DOI will use the risk calculations to prioritize the National Critical NMI assets to facilitate appropriate implementation of protective measures and program requirements. DOI will conduct risk calculations for its own facilities and encourage other asset owners to implement the methodology presented herein for those NMI assets not owned or operated by DOI.

3.4.1 Assessing Security System Effectiveness

In the initial step of the risk assessment process, a standard VA approach is used to identify security weaknesses of the asset. The weaknesses are determined based on an assessment of the effectiveness of the asset's existing security systems and procedures to prevent or mitigate the specified attack or hazard scenarios being considered. In order to measure each security system's effectiveness against a specific scenario, "effectiveness" has been divided into five levels, each of which is assigned a corresponding point value ranging from 0.1 to 0.9. For example, if an assessment of the asset's vulnerability to an IED attack determines that existing security systems and procedures are likely to prevent or mitigate the attack to a level resulting in little or no damage, the system would be considered Fully Effective and assigned a point value of 0.9. See table 3-3 for a description of the effectiveness characteristics of the security system.

Table 3-3: Security System Effectiveness

Security System Effectiveness	Security System Characteristics	Point Value
Fully Effective [Very High]	The system presents an obstacle expected to prevent an adversary from achieving the attack scenario objective or the natural hazard from compromising the structure.	0.9
Effective [High]	The system presents an obstacle that would require a high level of effort to overcome in order for an adversary to achieve the attack scenario objective or minimizes the impact of the natural hazard.	0.7
Somewhat Effective [Moderate]	The system presents an obstacle that would require moderate effort to overcome in order for an adversary to achieve the attack scenario objective or under certain circumstances the natural hazard could affect the structure.	0.5
Minimally Effective [Low]	The system presents an obstacle that would require minimal effort to overcome in order for an adversary to achieve the attack scenario objective or the natural hazard would almost always compromise the structure.	0.3
Ineffective [Very Low]	The system presents no obstacle to prevent an adversary from achieving the attack scenario objective or the natural hazard having an adverse impact.	0.1

3.4.2 Gauging the Likelihood of Successful Attack or Hazard

After establishing the effectiveness of the security systems to prevent or mitigate the specified attack or hazard scenarios, the assessment process gauges the likelihood of success for each scenario. This is accomplished by establishing the likelihood of a specific attack or hazard occurring and the effectiveness (or ineffectiveness) of the security system to protect against that scenario. In order to develop a baseline risk value, it is assumed that each of the specified scenarios is credible and has an equal probability of occurrence. Given this parameter, the likelihood of an adversary successfully executing a specific attack scenario or of a natural hazard being realized can essentially be measured as the inverse of the Security System Effectiveness point value for that scenario.

$$\text{Likelihood of Successful Attack or Hazard} = 1 - \text{System Effectiveness} \rightarrow L_A = (1 - S_E)$$

For example, if the asset's security system is considered Fully Effective (a point value of 0.9) against an attack scenario, the likelihood of a successful attack being carried out would be considered Very Low (a point value of 0.1).

The point values assigned to the System Effectiveness and Likelihood of Successful Attack or Hazard categories are developed using available documentation, concurrent site surveys, interviews with security personnel familiar with the asset and its operation, and onsite reviews. These resources provide the survey team with a snapshot of the asset's current security posture from which to assess each scenario.

3.4.3 Calculating Risk Values

Once the effectiveness of the asset's security systems and the likelihood of successful attack or compromise by a natural hazard have been determined for each scenario, the process of calculating risk values can proceed. Using the Total Consequence Value developed for each scenario during the Consequence Assessment Phase (section 3.3) and the corresponding values for the Likelihood of Successful Attack or Hazard (section 3.4.2), the risk associated with each scenario can be quantified. The Risk Value is derived by multiplying the Total Consequence Value by its corresponding Likelihood of Successful Attack or Hazard Value.

$$\text{Risk Value} = \text{Likelihood of Successful Attack or Hazard} \times \text{Total Consequence Value} \rightarrow R_{TS} = L_A (1 - S_E) \times C_{\text{Attack Scenario Total}}$$

As a final step, the risk values for each scenario are added together to derive the asset's Overall Risk Value. The Overall Risk Value can be translated into a corresponding asset vulnerability rating of High, Medium, or Low. The Overall Risk Value provides a means of evaluating the effects of improvements such as security hardware enhancements, operational changes, and staffing increases in reducing an asset's vulnerabilities and allows for the relative ranking of all NMI assets. Overall Risk Value can be calculated using table 3-4.

The System Effectiveness, Likelihood of Successful Attack or Hazard, Total Consequence Value, and Risk Value can be shown in the table. Combining these factors produces the Overall Risk Value score.

Table 3-4: Overall Risk Value

Attack Scenario	System Effectiveness	Likelihood of Successful Attack or Hazard	Total Consequence Value	Risk Value
	$S_E + L_A (1-S_E) \times C_{\text{Attack Scenario Total}} = R_{TS}$			
			Overall Risk Value for Asset	

3.5 Assessing Threats

The threat scenarios considered for the NMI Sector are high level and are considered applicable for all assets. The threat of each potential attack scenario is based on an understanding of the adversary's intent and an assessment of the adversary's capability. Similar considerations drive the analysis of natural hazards.

Although a general threat underlies the sector due to the open accessibility of NMI assets, each asset has its own distinct vulnerabilities due to location, surrounding geography, structure, and so on. Close collaboration with responsible law enforcement and security personnel is necessary to facilitate understanding and assessing the threat level faced.

DOI will work internally to capture any threats to the sector utilizing various resources. The DHS Homeland Infrastructure Threat and Risk Analysis Center (HITRAC), for example, provides various reports to the SSA that present sector-specific terrorist threat information. Other products include CIKR asset-specific intelligence and trend analysis as it relates to the sector's critical infrastructure. DOI also utilizes eGuardian and National Counterterrorism Center related products that contribute to the general threat environment.

4. Prioritize Infrastructure

When a determination is made that an asset belongs within the NMI Sector, the first step in the prioritization process is to place the asset into a specific tier level bin (National Critical, National Significant, Regional Critical, or Local Significant) as described in section 3.2. To date, DOI has completed this initial prioritization. As the sector matures, the NMI GCC will be responsible for determining the bin into which an asset falls.

DOI will subject assets designated as National Critical to the NMI risk assessment methodologies described in sections 3.3 and 3.4 to develop a numerical score based on the consequences and vulnerabilities of each asset. DOI will conduct the assessment for those assets it owns and will work with the owners of other assets to ensure that the assessment is conducted. Cyber considerations for this sector are minimal; however, they are treated as an integral part of each asset and handled as part of the overall asset prioritization.

DOI will work through the NMI GCC and with the Government Facilities Sector to ensure that owners of assets categorized as National Significant, Regional Critical, and Local Significant have access to the methodology. DOI will not assist in the actual assessments due to staffing and funding limitations.

Once priorities are established, they will become the basis for resource allocation and protective program development.

Reassessments of DOI-owned National Critical assets will be conducted on a biannual basis. In the event that the security posture changes significantly, a reassessment may be conducted to accurately address any new risks.

5. Develop and Implement Protective Programs and Resilience Strategies

5.1 Overview of Sector Protective Programs and Resilience Strategies

The NMI Sector has several distinguishing risk management characteristics that aid in defining the sector's end state:

- The sector's structures, locations, and artifacts are recognized worldwide as unique historical and cultural symbols of American values, history, and national identity. Many of these assets are inherently irreplaceable, physically and psychologically, and a successful terrorist attack on the sector could have dramatic consequences for public morale. Accordingly, the risk management focus in the sector is heavily weighted toward prevention and protection.

- NMI assets are typically stand-alone assets or sites located in urban and rural settings, such as bridges, ships, documents, artwork, monuments, estates, and mountains. Although the assets are by nature static and defined (e.g., the Washington Monument), the environment surrounding the asset is dynamic (e.g., the National Mall) and, therefore, challenging from a security standpoint. Operational and protective requirements may also vary depending on the season and/or occurrence of a special event.

- NMI assets must be open to the public and attention must be paid to preserve the historic or artistic value of the site as a whole. Protective measures are thus set in the context of community standards on accessibility and the desire to maintain the aesthetics of the site. The intrinsically public nature of the sector and the limitations imposed on its protective measures increase the challenges of protecting NMI assets.

- Monuments and icons attract large numbers of visitors and present attractive targets for adversaries. Protective measures must ensure the security of the site itself and plan for the safety of visitors in an emergency situation.

- National icons may also serve other critical infrastructure needs and fall primarily under the protective domain of other sectors (e.g., Hoover Dam is under the oversight of the Dams Sector, while the Sears Tower is classified in the Commercial Facilities Sector).

- Funding for public safety and security programs generally comes from operational funds, especially for those assets owned by DOI.

5.2 Determining Protective Program Needs

Because of the highly distributed nature of the assets in the NMI Sector, the responsibility for protection is shared among affected Federal, State, local, and tribal governments, as well as the private sector. DOI, key stakeholders, and asset-specific law enforcement have developed and implemented protective programs on an accelerated basis since the attacks on September 11th. A mix of new regulations, congressional mandates, actual and perceived threat information, and vulnerabilities is driving these programs. DOI's approach to protecting natural and historic sites and 1.3 million visitors daily provides a solid foundation for the NMI protection program. NMI is unique because although the destruction of an NMI asset would surely cause some form of psychosocial impact, it most likely would not affect any other sectors in their operation. The Office of Law Enforcement and Security, specifically the Security Division, addresses the Physical Protection and Facility Security format within the 444 Department Manual 1, which gives the guidelines for NMI security and protection. There is no official DOI guidance on resilience of assets, and restoration or recovery would most likely be addressed by DOI senior management on a situation-specific basis. The following three capabilities can be leveraged to address other sector assets:

- Experience DOI gained in conducting risk-based VAs on iconic national monuments, including threat assessments and recommended security upgrades;

- Significant experience in identifying, implementing, and evaluating physical protection strategies for visitors to national parks; and

- Access to VAs, security plans, and response plans from law enforcement agencies that are currently protecting some of the high-risk NMI assets.

DOI, in consultation with DHS, is following a systematic, threat-based approach to develop protective programs across the entire sector.

In addition, many of the sector partners have programs in place to mitigate the effects of an all-hazards type incident that may impact their assets. DOI, through several of its bureaus, is heavily involved in monitoring earthquakes and volcanoes, and works closely with several other Federal agencies to track hurricanes. A wide spectrum of Federal, State, local, and tribal government agencies, as well as the private sector, routinely share this information.

Assets within the NMI Sector are owned by the Federal Government, and the Federal budget process is the sole source for appropriated funding. Federal managers must determine the cost-benefit ratio of implementing a security measure and/or protective program versus the risk associated with not expending those funds. If the risk is determined to be acceptable, in many cases the funding is used for other priorities.

The public nature of the NMI Sector limits the range of protective measures available. As a result, NMI Sector assets have unique protection challenges compared with other sectors. NMI Sector assets are generally open to the public and must preserve the historic footprint of the site. A diverse range of vehicle types is often grouped in or near NMI Sector assets. Depending on the site, automobiles, recreational vehicles, boats, trailers, and service and concessionaire delivery vehicles may be parked within the perimeter of the asset or in close proximity. Sector partners recognize the significant threat posed by IEDs and VBIEDs. In recent years, these have been the preferred attack methods of terrorists. Although many measures have been taken to "harden" facilities against these types of attacks, significant vulnerabilities remain because of the potential size and range of these devices.

5.3 Protective Program Implementation

DOI recognizes the need for a systematic approach in developing protective programs to ensure a consistent, efficient, and effective level of protection across the NMI Sector. In addition, DOI is responsible for most assets within the sector designated as National Critical and has a long history and extensive experience in protecting NMI assets.

DOI will use a methodical, disciplined approach to match available resources with National Critical NMI assets and share validated protective measures currently in use throughout DOI with other stakeholders. Because National Critical NMI assets crosscut different Federal agencies, the participation of all entities is paramount to ensuring the highest level of protection for our Nation's NMI assets.

DOI has developed a chapter in its departmental manual that describes the minimum required protective measures that must be in place at all DOI-owned critical infrastructure (see appendix 3). The standards capture best practices from a security perspective and outline minimum recommended measures for each asset. The Department has identified baseline physical security standards as well as additional, more rigorous standards for implementation as the threat or hazard level against an asset or the sector increases.

NMI assets are designed to attract and encourage visitation. Security at NMI assets must be unobtrusive and flexible to accommodate large numbers of visitors but still provide security commensurate with the level of risk identified. Following completion of the vulnerability and risk assessments (as discussed in chapter 3), DOI will continue to coordinate development and implementation of physical security protection for NMI assets.

DOI will do the following:

- Identify security strengths and weaknesses based on asset characteristics;

- Evaluate risks based on seasonal and holiday considerations and adjacent critical infrastructures;

- Develop a matrix with asset characteristics and vulnerabilities;

- Develop risk-prioritized listing of sector assets to facilitate application of protective measures using a graded approach;

- Develop a set of minimum security standards for each tier of NMI assets; and

- Develop a set of recommended security enhancements for elevated threat or alert levels.

DOI leadership will determine whether the risk assessments warrant action and whether the recommended courses of action are feasible based on available resources and other factors. At this juncture, the risks associated with DOI-owned NMI assets are known, and the decision concerning what level of risk is acceptable will be made.

Because many NMI assets are not owned by the Federal Government, and there is no regulatory authority to require compliance with protective program measures, DOI will work with DHS and other agencies to promote cooperation and involvement of stakeholders in implementing this plan. The SSA's role under this initiative is to share information with stakeholders and encourage involvement.

Because many NMI assets are located in urban settings and have become an integral part of the fabric of city life, a critical component of the decisionmaking process is to develop a strong dialogue with civic leaders, community groups, historic preservation officials, architects, and others regarding the proposed measures.

The following are examples of security-related measures that have been implemented at DOI-owned assets to improve protective measures by leveraging scarce resources:

- DOI officials at the Statue of Liberty have partnered with DoD research units to test emerging technologies that may eventually be used to protect military personnel and facilities. The partnership has provided the Statue of Liberty with cutting-edge protective technology at no cost to DOI and has facilitated product testing in a real-world application.

- DOI officials at Mount Rushmore National Monument have manipulated the natural landscape palette to augment the existing perimeter control barrier surrounding the asset. They have leveraged the passive use of the physical environment to effectively reduce the risk of a VBIED attack at the asset.

- DOI officials at NMI assets are incorporating appropriate security awareness messages in printings of park newspapers and brochures disseminated to visitors.

The following paragraphs describe broad protective measures and programs in all facets of the security spectrum.

Awareness

DOI has assessed risk, vulnerability, and threat information for DOI-owned assets to establish a readiness standard. In addition, with stakeholder participation, DOI will catalog critical NMI assets, including their vulnerabilities across the threat spectrum.

Prevention/Protection

DOI's prevention and protection strategy is based on employing best practices, developing standards, providing guidance, and issuing internal DOI security directives. DOI will share the best practices, standards, lessons learned, and other aspects developed through stakeholder interaction. DOI also may conduct annual exercises at DOI-owned assets to test specific plans and to assess the strength, viability, and level of preparedness. DOI will use a readiness assessment system to measure the industry's security posture in response to the threat level established by DHS.

Specific Protective Measures

DOI will develop a menu of protective items to facilitate selecting the best protective practices applicable to a specific situation. The process will be as open as possible to enable the individual asset owners and operators to select the solution best tailored to their needs based on the results of the risk assessments conducted for their assets.

- Protective measures can be specific to a single asset or applicable across the sector. DOI will ensure that there is crosscut among types of NMI assets to ensure maximum use of these specific measures and sharing of best practices;

- Measures will be best practices within the industry that properly weigh risk avoidance or mitigation against cost; and

- Measures will be communicated via planning guidance issued by industry, the private sector, and other relevant entities.

Security Plans

DOI will coordinate the structure and maintenance of security plans for DOI-owned NMI assets to ensure consistency and compatibility. Plans will address domain awareness, prevention, preparedness, response, and recovery efforts. DOI will provide guidance to stakeholders to encourage functional equivalency within the asset category and consistency with the National Response Framework (NRF) and the National Incident Management System (NIMS) when preparing plans.

- DOI will develop risk-based plans for its internal assets.

- DOI will conduct rigorous plan reviews for DOI-owned assets. For other National Critical assets, DOI will provide assistance to other Federal agencies in reviewing plans and recommendations for improvements. For assets categorized as National Significant, Regional Critical, and Local Significant, DOI will encourage certification within the framework of the program and work with DHS and the GCC to develop mechanisms for sharing information within the sector.

- A portion of the protection and mitigation measures for NMI assets are borne by owners outside of DOI and must be considered when developing programs. DOI will consider the use of conferences, symposiums, public forums, and stakeholder outreach when crafting programs.

Protection of Supporting Infrastructure

DOI will coordinate with DHS in protecting other infrastructure that support NMI assets (e.g., cyber, power, and telecommunications) or are the responsibility of DHS or another sector. Based on guidance from DHS, DOI will provide this information to NMI asset owners as part of its guidance on implementing protective programs for the sector.

SSA Relationships With State and Local Agencies

State and local authorities may be the first on the scene of an attack on an NMI asset. DOI will work closely with Federal officials and regional preparedness agencies in coordinating recovery efforts and restoring public confidence after an attack on a DOI-owned NMI asset. State and local authorities constitute the front line of defense for some of DOI's critical assets, and in some cases, are the owners or operators of a historic landmark. Public safety agencies such as law enforcement, fire/rescue, emergency medical services, and emergency management are an integral part of prevention, mitigation, response, and recovery.

Resource Management

To effectively coordinate actions to prevent, deter, and mitigate attacks on an NMI asset, awareness of the security resources available across the Federal, State, and local governments; Territories; and private sector jurisdictions is critical. Developed under the requirements of HSPD-5, the NRF outlines the mechanisms for resource sharing at the Federal, State, and local levels. These mechanisms include memoranda of agreement, mutual aid agreements, mutual aid pacts, and similar protocols. Federal resources can be deployed to temporarily provide protection to critical national infrastructure. During high threat conditions, DOI and DHS may coordinate deployment.

Response Preparedness

Preparedness encompasses actions taken before a terrorist attack or all-hazards incident occurs and includes pre-staging resources, exercising with first responders, and planning for restoration of NMI assets.

Response preparedness also presumes that despite best efforts, an attack or all-hazards incident may still occur. DOI will coordinate efforts with multiple jurisdictions as necessary, including Federal, State, and local stakeholders; nongovernmental organizations; and the private sector if an attack or all-hazards incident occurs at a DOI-owned asset. In addition, DOI will work with the Federal Bureau of Investigation (FBI) and other law enforcement agencies to investigate the cause of the incident, protect any evidence, and use the information to improve prevention measures.

Response Plans

DOI will use NIMS to manage a response to an attack in accordance with HSPD-5. NIMS will provide unity of command, a manageable span of control, the use of common terminology, and a scalable management structure to mitigate the immediate effects of an attack. If an incident occurs, DOI will coordinate with the Principal Federal Official with incident response. DOI will also conduct an investigation of the event to identify areas where response preparedness and prevention standards could be strengthened.

Cybersecurity Considerations

The February 2003 presidential report National Strategy to Secure Cyberspace provides DOI with a framework for approaching cybersecurity for the NMI Sector. IT and telecommunication networks directly support the operation of all sectors of our economy, including energy (electric power, oil, gas), transportation (highway, rail, air, maritime), finance and banking, information and communications, public health, emergency services, water, chemical, defense industrial base, food and agriculture, and postal and shipping services.

The cyber threat has been identified as a potential attack scenario for all sectors to consider. IT and telecommunication systems are important to the operations of a limited number of NMI assets, and an attack on those systems could possibly affect the availability, function, or mission of an asset but not necessarily impact other sectors.

DOI will consider the following principles for protecting IT and telecommunication systems, whether used operationally or for physical security:

• Reduce cyber threats and deter malicious actors through effective programs to identify and punish them;

- Identify and address those existing vulnerabilities that could create the most damage to critical systems if exploited;

- Develop new systems with less vulnerability and assess emerging technologies for vulnerabilities; and

- Initiate workforce surety measures through implementation of a standard identity credential for secure and reliable identification and authentication of Federal Government employees and contractors as specified in Federal Information Processing Standards (FIPS) Publication 201 and its supporting authorities.

The implementation of these principles into the protection program will include four major actions:

- Enhance cybersecurity awareness training programs;

- Reduce cyber vulnerabilities;

- Respond to cybersecurity threats; and

- Establish NMI cybersecurity working groups.

5.4 Monitoring Program Implementation

DOI continues to monitor protective programs at DOI-owned assets on a continual basis, and formal vulnerability reassessments of National Critical NMI assets on a biannual basis utilizing set procedures within the 444 DM 2, Physical Protection and Facility Security, to determine which protective programs are successful.

DOI establishes the security requirements necessary to minimally safeguard departmental CIKR assets and to also assist owners and operators of non-DOI-owned assets in periodically assessing their protective measures and posture. Guidance includes:

1. Ensuring the national CIKR assets which they own and/or control are identified and inventoried.

2. Conducting periodic reviews of its designated national CIKR inventory to ensure the appropriate assets are identified in light of current guidance and changing threat environments.

3. Ensuring the requirements set forth in this chapter are implemented at the national CIKR asset(s) which they own and/or operate.

DOI continues to improve the communication of efforts and progress of the sector through the Security Division's annual training seminar. Last year's training was held at NASA and hosted several partners from the GCC and outside public community.

DOI's continued working relationship with DHS's S&T has helped to determine specific needs for assets. DOI looks forward to the continued support of S&T in the initiatives, such as the testing/experimenting of magnetometer methods held at the Statue of Liberty.

6. Measure Effectiveness

The NMI Sector's approach to measuring effectiveness of sector activities is to coordinate with programs established by sector partners. This approach is reflected in the Sector Annual Report (SAR). In particular, appendix B of the SAR lists the sector's risk mitigation activities (RMAs). The remainder of this chapter describes the process DOI and sector partners use to measure effectiveness through the use of progress indicators.

6.1 Risk Mitigation Activities

This section describes the process the NMI Sector uses to develop the RMAs that result from its protective programs and resilience strategies identified in chapter 5 of this SSP. These RMAs will support the achievement of overall CIKR protection goals and the primary sector goal of ensuring those National Critical NMI assets remain intact and accessible to the public at all times (or are not closed for security reasons). DOI will use these goals as the standard to measure progress and will direct resources toward those activities that best support accomplishing the goals. Activities that do not advance the goals will be redesigned or eliminated over time. Furthermore, the goals have evolved and will continue to evolve as the sector matures.

NMI metrics will focus on monitoring progress within the sector. The metrics discussed below are expected to evolve as DHS and sector partners gain additional experience with their specific CIKR protection programs and resilience challenges.

DOI and its sector partners have identified multiple RMAs in the NMI SAR. Appendix B of the SAR lists key RMAs and progress indicators, as well as the sector's other RMAs. For each of the key RMAs, the SAR identifies descriptive data, output data, and outcome metrics. The key RMAs generally are assessment programs administered by DOI and sector partners that yield outcome and other quantifiable metrics that can be reported on an annual basis. The other RMAs are programs, methodologies, and partnerships (e.g., Buffer Zone Protection Program (BZPP)) that assist with security efforts at NMI assets but that may not be sufficiently quantifiable or continuing over time to qualify as a key RMA.

6.2 Process for Measuring Effectiveness

6.2.1 Process for Measuring Sector Progress

DOI has worked closely with its sector partners to align outcome-based metrics to sector goals and objectives and to develop a process for measuring progress. For example, DOI coordinates with its GCC partners annually to update asset information contained in the IDW. This process helps inform progress measurement by collecting output and descriptive data on an annual basis.

DOI has created data and metrics to establish progress indicators that measure the sector's performance in protecting NMI assets. One initiative that DOI selected to accomplish this goal is protective systems assessments at NMI Sector assets. DOI has encouraged the GCC partners to perform protective systems assessments at their CIKR using the NMI assessment methodology described in chapter 3 of this SSP. These assessments, which monitor the effectiveness of specific protective measures, further the sector goal of improving protection of NMI assets.

An important element of DOI's approach for measuring effectiveness has been to leverage existing infrastructure resilience programs of sector partners. This has allowed greater coverage in measuring progress across sector assets. For example, the SI is responsible for protecting staff, visitors, national collections, and facilities entrusted to it. The Smithsonian's anti-terrorism program reports to DOI on the number of security assessments completed and/or initiated during the reporting year, among other metrics.

Over time, DOI will place increased emphasis on the outcome-based metrics component to provide greater focus on ensuring progress.

The metrics do not specifically address cyber components of NMI assets because these are integral to the vulnerability analyses and protective programs and are not separate assets themselves. If cyber issues become a significant factor for the NMI Sector, then appropriate metrics will be added.

6.2.2 Information Collection and Verification

For DOI-owned assets, the Department's Office of Law Enforcement and Security coordinates with the National Park Service and U.S. Park Police to collect pertinent metrics information and verify its accuracy.

For non-DOI-owned Federal Government assets, DOI works with the responsible Federal agency on collection and verification of the metrics information. For example, the National Archives Security Management Branch is responsible for the full range of physical, personnel, and information security and protection at NARA facilities. NARA reports its progress on outcome metrics (e.g., number of security assessments completed during the reporting year) to DOI on an annual basis. DOI relies on NARA to verify the information that it collects. Similarly, for data regarding progress indicators collected by other CIKR partners (e.g., SI), the other partner takes responsibility not only for collecting the data, but also for verifying its accuracy. DOI coordinates with sector partners to ensure that satisfactory data verification processes are in place and implemented.

6.2.3 Reporting

Each year, DOI updates the information in the sector metrics prior to the annual deadline for reporting sector CIKR data. The information is gathered internally, through the GCC, and with the assistance of sector partners. DOI compiles and reports the information to DHS in accordance with DHS guidance, e.g., by listing the RMAs and providing descriptive data, output data, and outcome metrics for each in the NMI SAR. This information is reported back to the sector partners through the SAR.

6.3 Using Metrics for Continuous Improvement

Significant progress has been made within this sector since the September 11th attacks. Using metrics to improve performance is a continuing process whereby past results can be measured, monitored, and decisions made on how to proceed with ongoing efforts. Metrics can assist with guiding the sector and providing opportunities to develop new ideas for improving implementation of the NIPP risk management framework.

The metrics described previously in this chapter will help determine where funding should be focused to achieve measurable and justifiable improvements. For example, if insufficient progress is made going forward on specific RMAs, funding for these efforts can be re-programmed to RMAs showing a greater return on invested funds in terms of progress against goals. More specifically, the process for addressing insufficient progress on vulnerabilities identified for an individual asset is through the assessments implemented by DOI's Security Division on a biannual basis. The report of these assessments is generated and forwarded to the decisionmakers for incorporation into their budget.

The processes identified above for reporting on sector-specific metrics, as well as SSA requirements for reporting progress will continue. DOI and sector partners will focus on ways to continually improve the accuracy of the information provided under these mechanisms and its usefulness in achieving sector goals.

7. CIKR Protection Research and Development

7.1 Overview of Sector R&D

Federal R&D planning for CIKR protection is based on the NIPP and HSPD-7, which states the following:

> *"In coordination with the Director of the Office of Science and Technology Policy, the Secretary shall prepare, on an annual basis, a Federal Research and Development Plan in support of this directive."*

In addition to the NIPP, HSPD-7 establishes an annual requirement for the National Critical Infrastructure Protection Research and Development Plan (NCIP R&D Plan). DHS S&T supports the Secretary of Homeland Security by preparing the annual long-term vision plan, set out in three strategic goals:

- A common operating picture to continuously monitor the health of CIKR;
- A next-generation Internet architecture with designed-in security; and
- Resilient, self-diagnosing, self-healing infrastructure systems.

HSPD-7 also instructs OSTP and DHS to coordinate interagency R&D to enhance the protection of CIKR. Planning needs to be collaborative so cross-sector priorities can be identified and R&D solutions developed to meet the needs of a specific infrastructure sector. The NCIP R&D Plan has nine research theme areas:

- Detection and Sensor Systems;
- Protection and Prevention;
- Entry and Access Portals;
- Insider Threats;
- Analysis and Decision Support Systems;
- Response and Recovery Tools;
- New and Emerging Threats and Vulnerabilities;
- Advanced Infrastructure Architectures and System Designs; and
- Human and Social Issues.

DOI continues to work with DHS's S&T to determine significant new technology that would benefit NMI assets.

7.2 Sector R&D Requirements

Assets included in the NMI Sector offer challenges to effective security enhancement due to factors such as maintaining public access, recognition, and visitation. Emerging technologies may help enhance security for these assets.

However, due to concerns over terrorist activity and the need for enhanced protection equipment, commercial off-the-shelf (COTS) security equipment may not serve as a solution to reduce vulnerabilities to terrorism. DOI will continue to collaborate with DHS and OSTP to stay abreast of the multivariate threats to NMI assets and work in concert to build an understanding of needed R&D in security measures, COTS, and emerging technologies that may assist in reducing associated known gaps.

Primary technology requirements for the NMI Sector are for unobtrusive surveillance, screening, and interdiction security technologies that maintain the aesthetic qualities of the assets without taking away the enhanced security when required. These requirements may include any of the following:

- Technologies for maintaining a controlled perimeter;
- Unobtrusive surveillance techniques, including biometric technology to include internal and external security technologies (e.g., buried lines, seismic pressure sensors, magnetic sensors, electric field sensors, coaxial cable, passive infrared technology, chemical/biological/radiological sensors, face recognition technology, algorithm closed-circuit television (CCTV) technology) that meet the physical security objectives of the protection program strategies;
- Research projects that develop unobtrusive physical security technologies through environmental design, and studies that provide innovative ways to protect NMI assets; and
- Automated suspicious behavior studies, intent determination, and anomalous behavior monitoring.

7.3 Sector R&D Plan

Physical protection R&D projects are needed to develop standardized methodologies and decision aids for VAs as well as to introduce new approaches for protecting elements critical to assets and infrastructure. These elements include the asset and control centers, power generation and transmission systems, and transportation and communication systems. DOI will evaluate and incorporate R&D of new technologies into the implementation of new equipment and the development of common standards and best practices.

The DOI liaison from the NMI Sector will confer with DHS/S&T and OSTP on a periodic basis to identify current Federal R&D initiatives that may be applicable to the sector. DOI will share this information with sector stakeholders through the GCC to gather input relative to those initiatives of most value to the sector.

NMI Sector assets qualify in some ways as facilities or locations that have physical security needs similar to those of other sectors and therefore are aligned with many of the efforts outlined in the NCIP R&D Plan. However, except for the safety of visitors at NMI locations, the consideration for protection of these assets is not related to services rendered or products produced, but rather to the damage to the national psyche if they were to be damaged or lost. In addition, because they have no explicit service or product output and minimal interdependency with sectors other than the Government Facilities Sector, their connection to the three strategic goals of the NCIP is limited. However, most NMI Sector assets represent unique protection challenges because of their location, age, design, and the general need for them to remain open and accessible.

Some examples of emerging technology initiatives that are in use for evaluation at NMI Sector assets are as follows:

- RedXDefense Incident Management System;
- ICX Technology FIDO—handheld detector for trinitrotoluene (TNT)-based explosives; and
- CX Technology FIDO Fast Gate—covert detector of trace TNT-based explosives.

R&D projects that the NMI Sector is following include but are not limited to the following:

- BioWatch Generation 3 Detection Systems;

- Detect-to-Protect Triggers and Confirmers;

- Detect-to-Protect Remote Sensors;

- Autonomous Rapid Facility Chemical Agent Monitor;

- Lightweight Autonomous Chemical Identification System;

- Next-Generation Biological Agent Detector;

- Next-Generation Chemical Warfare Agent and High-Priority Toxic Industrial Chemical Detector;

- Homemade Explosive Performance Determination, Damage Effects, Modeling, and Simulation;

- Blast/Projectile-Unified Blast Analysis Tools and Protective Measures; and

- Waterside Blast Analysis Tools, Protective Measures, and Vetting of Underwater Blast Effects Codes.

7.4 R&D Management Processes

DOI continues to manage and/or govern the sector R&D through a collaborative process with the GCC partners and remains accountable, ensuring proper information sharing across the sector Homeland Security Information Network (HSIN) portal.

Coordination with the CIP R&D remains a high priority in order to ensure that future projects are focused on preventing or mitigating threats to computer networks and are an important aspect of the operation and safety of NMI assets. As the SSA, DOI confers both with DHS/S&T and OSTP and with other like sectors on a periodic basis to identify current Federal R&D initiatives that may be applicable to the sector. DOI provides GCC partners with information concerning ongoing R&D projects that may affect the sector, as well as the universe of ongoing and planned DHS/Federal R&D initiatives.

Assets within the NMI Sector are owned by the Federal Government, and the Federal budget process is the sole source for appropriated funding. Federal managers must determine the cost-benefit ratio of implementing a security measure versus the risk associated with not expending those funds. If the risk is determined to be acceptable, in many cases the funding is used for other priorities.

8. Managing and Coordinating SSA Responsibilities

8.1 Program Management Approach

As the SSA for the NMI Sector, DOI has been unable to create a separate program office to manage NIPP-related responsibilities due to limitations on staffing and funding.

Within DOI, the SSA responsibility is delegated to a Security Specialist assigned in the Security Division of the Office of Law Enforcement and Security. When necessary, the Assistant Director of the Security Division acts as the secondary point of contact. As appropriate and necessary, they will work closely with other personnel assigned primarily with the NPS and the U.S. Park Police, which are the two agencies within DOI with primary responsibility for NMI assets.

8.2 Processes and Responsibilities

8.2.1 SSP Maintenance and Update

As the SSA, DOI works with the GCC to determine when a change within the sector warrants updating the SSP. In addition, while compiling the annual report with the GCC partners, DOI will highlight any outstanding issues that may warrant changes. DOI will discuss proposed changes with all GCC partners and seek their concurrence prior to implementation.

DOI will review the SSP and update it triennially in conjunction with the review of the NIPP in coordination with DHS.

8.2.2 SSP Implementation Milestones

DOI sees the milestones as one and the same with the priorities the sector would like to achieve.

- **Priority 1:** Develop unobtrusive physical security techniques and/or environmental/architectural designs that enhance perimeter security; cost-effective visitor screening technology that maintains accessibility and/or unobtrusive surveillance; and reliable chemical, biological, radiological, nuclear, and explosive detection systems.

- **Priority 2:** Continue to encourage DHS to complete a comprehensive study of the psychosocial impacts of a terrorist attack on an NMI asset. A pilot study was conducted by the Homeland Security Institute (HSI) in 2008.

- **Priority 3:** Complete blast assessments at NMI Sector assets.

- **Priority 4:** Support workforce surety through the implementation of a standard identity credential for secure and reliable identification and authentication of Federal Government employees and contractors, as specified in Federal Information Processing Standards Publication 201 and its supporting authorities.

- **Priority 5:** Implement civil aviation restrictions around CIKR assets located outside of the Washington, D.C. metropolitan area.

- **Priority 6:** Participate in BZPP development and other security-related initiatives, such as the Lower Manhattan Security Initiative. In return, non-DHS Federal GCC partners would like to realize some benefit from their participation.

- **Priority 7:** Promote the use of the HSIN secure portal by GCC partners as a practical means of sharing information concerning physical and cyber threats, vulnerabilities, incidents, potential protective measures, and effective security practices.

- **Priority 8:** Continue to coordinate with the Government Facilities Sector in providing outreach to State, local, tribal, and private entities.

8.2.3 Resources and Budgets

Currently all assets identified within the NMI Sector are federally owned. Therefore, each department or agency within the sector will manage its own budget through the Federal budget process.

8.2.4 Training and Education

Successful implementation of the national risk management framework relies on building and maintaining individual and organizational expertise in CIKR protection. Training and education at a variety of levels and in a variety of subject areas are necessary to achieve and sustain an optimal level of expertise. Section 6.2 of the NIPP discusses some of the areas of expertise where training is recommended (e.g., individual, organizational, tabletop), as well as examples of the types of training currently being offered and other general information on training and education related to CIKR protection.

Individual and organizational training as well as tabletop exercises are integral to improving the NMI Sector's overall security posture. Training facility staff on how to identify suspicious activity could dramatically reduce the likelihood of a terrorist attack. DOI will encourage NMI Sector partners to participate in security-related training and educational opportunities. In addition, DOI will work with its partners to identify security-related training and educational opportunities.

8.3 Implementing the Partnership Model

8.3.1 NIPP Coordinating Councils

The sector partnership model is the framework proposed in the NIPP to promote and facilitate sector and cross-sector planning, coordination, collaboration, and information sharing for CIKR protection involving all levels of government and the private sector. The model encourages formation of GCCs to harmonize government efforts and SCCs to coordinate private sector efforts. DHS provides guidance, tools, and support to enable the councils to carry out their respective roles and responsibilities. The goals of the councils are to establish the context, framework, and support for activities required to implement and sustain the national CIKR protection effort.

8.3.2 NMI Sector SCC

The NMI Sector does not host an SCC due to the assets being federally owned; however, the sector has partnered with the Government Facilities Sector's GCC to provide outreach to State, local, and tribal entities. Information sharing with the NMI Sector GCC and from this body to the Government Facilities Sector's GCC will be facilitated through quarterly meetings and electronic message exchanges.

8.3.3 NMI Sector GCC

The NMI Sector GCC provides an effective mechanism for coordinating CIKR strategies and activities, policy, and communication across the government and between the government and the NMI Sector to support the Nation's homeland security mission.

The GCC will accomplish its objectives through the following activities:

- Identifying issues that require government coordination and communication. The GCC brings together diverse Federal and State interests to identify and develop collaborative strategies that advance critical infrastructure protection.
- Identifying needs and gaps in plans, programs, policies, procedures, and strategies.
- Acknowledging successful programs and practices. The GCC will facilitate the sharing of experiences, ideas, effective practices, and innovative approaches related to protecting critical infrastructure.
- Leveraging complementary resources within government and between government and industry.

The GCC meets quarterly or more frequently if required. The members of the NMI Sector GCC are representatives from the following agencies:

- U.S. Department of the Interior
  - Office of Law Enforcement and Security
  - National Park Service
  - U.S. Park Police
- Department of Homeland Security
  - Office of Infrastructure Protection
  - Federal Protective Service
  - U.S. Secret Service
- Department of Justice
  - Federal Bureau of Investigation
- Smithsonian Institution
- National Archives and Records Administration
- U.S. Capitol Police
- Department of Defense

8.4 Information Sharing and Protection

The lack of historical interactions within this sector, except for those assets owned by DOI, highlights the need for a structured method to disseminate information within the sector in a timely manner. This is a critical gap that needs to be addressed quickly across the entire sector.

Most sector assets rely on the information-sharing processes that the responsible law enforcement or security entity has in place. For critical operational information, the procedures currently in place within the law enforcement community should continue to be utilized and improved. The Critical Infrastructure Warning Information Network should be utilized as applicable. For sector-specific information of a less critical nature, the HSIN system should be used.

The NMI Sector developed its own HSIN portal to enable sector partners to share information quickly concerning threats and potential protective measures that have been used successfully. A key component of this information system will be the ability of DHS's HITRAC to quickly disseminate developing hazard or threat information or evolving patterns of attack to all NMI Sector partners.

The information used by the NMI Sector and its sector partners to manage risk and secure CIKR may contain sensitive data as well as proprietary or sensitive business information. As a result, information protection is a significant concern for those partners who are supplying this sensitive information. The NMI Sector will protect this information to the maximum extent possible.

Pursuant to the Critical Infrastructure Information Act of 2002, information that satisfies the requirements of the Act will be protected from public disclosure to the maximum extent permitted by law. The PCII Program managed by DHS is an out-growth of the Act. The rules governing the PCII Program are available at 6 CFR Part 29.

Appendix 1: List of Acronyms and Abbreviations

BOR	Bureau of Reclamation
C&A	Certification and Accreditation
CFR	Code of Federal Regulations
CIKR	Critical Infrastructure and Key Resources
CIO	Chief Information Officer
COTS	Commercial Off-the-Shelf
DHS	Department of Homeland Security
DoD	Department of Defense
DOI	Department of the Interior
DOJ	Department of Justice
FBI	Federal Bureau of Investigation
FIPS	Federal Information Processing Standards
FISMA	Federal Information Security Management Act
GCC	Government Coordinating Council
HITRAC	Homeland Infrastructure Threat and Risk Analysis Center
HSIN	Homeland Security Information Network
HSPD-7	Homeland Security Presidential Directive 7
IED	Improvised Explosive Device
IT	Information Technology
NARA	National Archives and Records Administration
NCSD	National Cyber Security Division
NIMS	National Incident Management System
NIPP	National Infrastructure Protection Plan
NIST	National Institute of Standards and Technology
NMI	National Monuments and Icons

NPS	National Park Service
NRF	National Response Framework
NSSE	National Special Security Event
OSTP	Office of Science and Technology Policy
PCII	Protected Critical Infrastructure Information
PSA	Protective Security Advisor
R&D	Research and Development
S&T	Science and Technology
SAR	Sector Annual Report
SBU	Sensitive But Unclassified
SCC	Sector Coordinating Council
SSA	Sector-Specific Agency
SSP	Sector-Specific Plan
USSS	U.S. Secret Service
VA	Vulnerability Assessment
VBIED	Vehicle-Borne Improvised Explosive Device

Appendix 2: Authorities

The assets currently identified as falling within the NMI Sector are all federally owned. These include a number of monuments and memorials under the jurisdiction of the NPS, a number of SI buildings, and the NARA building, including many of its contents. Most of these assets have their own dedicated law enforcement or security forces on site, but many rely on State or local law enforcement agencies to respond and provide support during special events or large incidents. It is imperative that the asset managers have agreements in place, preferably written, detailing the assistance available and the mechanics of how the assistance will flow in a smooth and orderly manner.

DOI, as the SSA, has no statutory or regulatory authority for collecting and sharing asset information (except for those assets under the NPS), completing vulnerability and risk assessments, or implementing protective programs. DOI must work with the asset owners, some of whom already have working relationships with bureaus within DOI, to gain voluntary compliance and cooperation.

The following specific authorities apply to the various partners of the NMI Sector:

- **DOI**

  - **Antiquities Act of 1906:** Congress passed the Antiquities Act of 1906, which authorized the President "to declare by public proclamation (as national monuments) historic landmarks, historic and prehistoric structures, and other objects of historic or scientific interest" (16 U.S.C. 431). The act also stated that any person who shall appropriate, excavate, injure, or destroy any historic monument without the permission of the Secretary of the Interior is in violation of Federal law.

  - **16 U.S.C. 1, National Park Service Organic Act:** In 1916, Congress created the NPS within DOI to "promote and regulate the use of the Federal areas known as national parks, monuments, and reservations." The interrelated provisions of the NPS Organic Act of 1916 established the NPS under DOI and the NPS General Authorities Act of 1970, including amendments to the latter law enacted in 1978 that reiterated the provisions of the Organic Act. The congressional report accompanying the 1978 amendment (Redwood Amendment) stated, "The Secretary has an absolute duty, which is not to be compromised, to fulfill the mandate of the 1916 Act to take whatever actions and seek whatever relief as will safeguard the units of the national park system."

  - **16 U.S.C. 1a-6, General Authorities Act of 1970 (Public Law 91-383, as amended by Public Law 94-458):** The Act stated the following: (a) The Secretary of the Interior (SOI) is authorized to designate, pursuant to standards prescribed in regulations by the Secretary, certain officer or employees of DOI who shall maintain law and order and protect persons and property within areas of the NPS. (b) SOI is hereby authorized to "designate officers and employees of any other Federal agency or law enforcement personnel of any State or political subdivision thereof, when deemed economical and in the public interest and with the concurrence of that agency or that State or subdivision, to act as special policemen in areas [of the National Park Service] when supplemental law enforcement personnel may be needed" and to exercise the powers and authority provided by paragraphs (1), (2), and (3) of subsection (a) of this section. On October 13, 1976, pursuant to 16 U.S.C. 1a-6 (b), the Director of the NPS designated "all United States Park Police officers to maintain law and order and protect persons and property within areas of the National Park System," as published in the Federal Register (41 FR 44876).

- **16 U.S.C. 1a-6, 43 U.S.C. 1733, 16 U.S.C. 7421, DOI Cross-Designation Agreements-Interagency Agreement:** "Pursuant to...Titles 16 U.S.C. 1a-6, 43 U.S.C. 1733, 16 U.S.C. 7421(b), 25 U.S.C. Chapter 30...it has been determined by all parties that the cross-designation of law enforcement officers [may be] mutually beneficial, economical, and advantageous to the public interest."

- **36 CFR 2.32:** 36 CFR 2.32 (a) (2) provides that authorized park employees may assert a lawful order to close or limit public access to park areas during law enforcement actions and emergency operations that involve a threat to public safety or park resources, or where the control of public movement and activities is necessary to maintain order and public safety.

- **16 U.S.C. 461, National Historic Sites Act of 1935:** This act declared it national policy to preserve for public use historic sites, buildings, and objects of national significance for the inspiration and benefit of the people of the United States. The regulation sets forth the criteria for establishing national significance and the procedures used by DOI for conducting the National Historic Landmarks Program.

- **16 U.S.C. 470, National Historic Preservation Act of 1966:** This act requires the Secretary of the Interior to promulgate regulations for the following: (1) approving and overseeing State historic preservation programs, (2) certifying local governments to carry out the purposes of the act, (3) ensuring that applicable State Historic Preservation Officers allocate a share of grants received under the act to certified local governments, and (4) assisting Indian tribes in preserving their particular historic properties.

- **Smithsonian Institution**

  - **40 U.S.C. 6301-6307:** This section provides the SI's Office of Protection Services the authority to police the buildings and grounds of the SI.

- **FBI**

  - **28 U.S.C. 533:** This section grants the FBI its investigative authority.

  - **USA PATRIOT Act:** This act granted the FBI new provisions to address the threat of terrorism.

- **USSS**

  - **U. S. Secret Service:** USSS was established as a law enforcement agency in 1865. Although most people associate the USSS with presidential protection, its original mandate was to investigate the counterfeiting of U.S. currency.

  - **18 U.S.C. 3056:** This authorizes agents and officers of the USSS to carry firearms; execute warrants issued under the laws of the United States; make arrests without warrants for any offense against the United States committed in their presence, or for any felony recognizable under the laws of the United States if they have reasonable grounds to believe that the person to be arrested has committed such felony; offer and pay rewards for services and information leading to the apprehension of persons involved in the violation of the law that the USSS is authorized to enforce; investigate fraud in connection with identification documents, fraudulent commerce, fictitious instruments and foreign securities; and perform other functions and duties authorized by law. The Secret Service works closely with the U.S. Attorney's Office in both protective and investigative matters.

  - **18 U.S.C. 871:** This authorizes the USSS to provide security for the President, the Vice President (or other individuals next in order of succession to the Office of the President), the President-elect, and Vice President-elect; the immediate families of the above individuals; former Presidents, their spouses for their lifetimes, except when the spouse remarries, and children of former presidents until age 16; visiting heads of foreign states or governments and their spouses traveling with them, other distinguished foreign visitors to the United States, and official representatives of the United States performing special missions abroad; and major presidential and vice presidential candidates and their spouses within 120 days of a general presidential election.

– **18 U.S.C. 1030:** This authorizes the USSS to safeguard the payment and financial systems of the United States. Historically, the USSS accomplished this through enforcement of the counterfeiting statutes to preserve the integrity of U.S. currency, coin, and financial obligations. Since 1984, the investigative responsibilities have expanded to include crimes that involve financial institution fraud, computer and telecommunications fraud, false identification documents, access device fraud, advance fee fraud, electronic funds transfers, and money laundering as it relates to USSS core violations.

Appendix 3: Minimum Security Requirements for DOI CIKR Assets

Security Personnel	
Minimum Requirement	Definition/Description
Dedicated/trained onsite Security Manager	Specific protective measures provided to NMI partners
360-degree visual coverage	Specific protective measures provided to NMI partners
24-hour presence	Specific protective measures provided to NMI partners
Periodic roving patrols	Specific protective measures provided to NMI partners
Armed security force	Specific protective measures provided to NMI partners
Reliable 24-hour communication system	Specific protective measures provided to NMI partners
Access to Explosive Ordnance Detection (EOD) K-9 unit on a 24-hour basis	Specific protective measures provided to NMI partners

Perimeter Security	
Minimum Requirement	Definition/Description
Physical perimeter with barriers preventing unauthorized vehicular access	Specific protective measures provided to NMI partners
Identification system and procedures for authorized parking within the security perimeter	Specific protective measures provided to NMI partners
Posted "No Parking" signs and arrangements for towing unauthorized vehicles	Specific protective measures provided to NMI partners
Closed-circuit television (CCTV) surveillance cameras (360-degree coverage)	Specific protective measures provided to NMI partners

Perimeter Security	
Minimum Requirement	**Definition/Description**
Monitoring the CCTV system on a 24-hour basis	Specific protective measures provided to NMI partners
External lighting with 360-degree coverage	Specific protective measures provided to NMI partners
Emergency lighting in critical areas	Specific protective measures provided to NMI partners
Lighting meets minimum standards for the CCTV system	Specific protective measures provided to NMI partners
Secure exterior utility systems and fuel sources	Specific protective measures provided to NMI partners

Access Control Security—Receiving/Shipping	
Minimum Requirement	**Definition/Description**
Review/implement receiving/shipping procedures	Specific protective measures provided to NMI partners
Restrict delivery access area to authorized personnel/vehicles	Specific protective measures provided to NMI partners
Post or secure receiving/shipping areas	Specific protective measures provided to NMI partners
Screen, search, and/or x-ray all incoming packages	Specific protective measures provided to NMI partners
Provide security training for all mailroom personnel	Specific protective measures provided to NMI partners

Access Control Security—Entrance/Exit	
Minimum Requirement	**Definition/Description**
Armed security personnel located (posted) at all open access points	Specific protective measures provided to NMI partners
X-ray and magnetometer equipment at public entrances with trained operators	Specific protective measures provided to NMI partners
Required inspection of vehicles entering the facility	Specific protective measures provided to NMI partners
Intrusion detection system (IDS) with 24-hour central monitoring capability	Specific protective measures provided to NMI partners
IDS using line supervision and backup power	Specific protective measures provided to NMI partners
IDS covering all access points	Specific protective measures provided to NMI partners

Access Control Security—Entrance/Exit	
Minimum Requirement	**Definition/Description**
HSPD-12-compliant card readers	Specific protective measures provided to NMI partners
Central database containing the location and serial numbers of all keys	Specific protective measures provided to NMI partners
High-security locks and secure door hinges	Specific protective measures provided to NMI partners

Interior Security	
Minimum Requirement	**Definition/Description**
Establish employee/contract employee identification authority	Specific protective measures provided to NMI partners
Agency photo ID for all employees displayed at all times	Specific protective measures provided to NMI partners
Visitor control system	Specific protective measures provided to NMI partners
Visitor identification accountability system	Specific protective measures provided to NMI partners
Secure interior utility areas	Specific protective measures provided to NMI partners
Emergency power for critical systems	Specific protective measures provided to NMI partners
Ability to close air intake system	Specific protective measures provided to NMI partners
Designated and trained occupant emergency plan official (refer to CFR 41-2.101-20.103.4)	Specific protective measures provided to NMI partners
Examine, update, and practice occupant emergency plans and contingency procedures once per year	Specific protective measures provided to NMI partners
Contacts for local police, fire department, hazardous materials teams, EOD team, etc.	Specific protective measures provided to NMI partners
All official computers in compliance with current DOJ security standards	Specific protective measures provided to NMI partners
Presence of a building emergency public address system	Specific protective measures provided to NMI partners
Established "shelter-in-place" plan	Specific protective measures provided to NMI partners

Security Planning	
Minimum Requirement	**Definition/Description**
Current law enforcement agency/security intelligence liaison contacts	Specific protective measures provided to NMI partners
Procedures in place for intelligence receipt/dissemination	Specific protective measures provided to NMI partners
Establish unusual facility incident reporting system	Specific protective measures provided to NMI partners
Conduct and document annual security awareness training for all employees	Specific protective measures provided to NMI partners
Standardized security force qualifications/training requirements	Specific protective measures provided to NMI partners
Implement/review construction projects for security enhancements	Specific protective measures provided to NMI partners
Establish employee access protocols	Specific protective measures provided to NMI partners
Establish security control procedures for service contract personnel	Specific protective measures provided to NMI partners